Paul Comon
Nikon N6000, N6006, N8008s

Magic Lantern Guides
Proof of Purchase
Nikon N6000, N6006,
N8008s

Paul Comon

Nikon

N6006 • N8008s • N6000

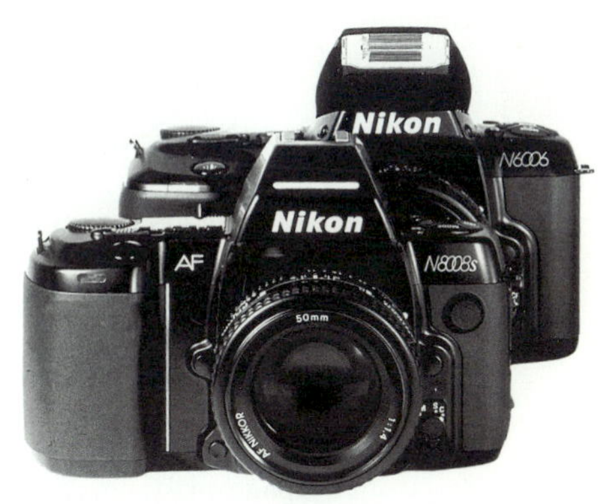

Laterna magica

Magic Lantern Guide to Nikon N6000, N6006, N8008s

A Laterna magica® book

Fifth Edition 1997
Published in the United States of America by

Silver Pixel Press
Divison of
The Saunders Group
21 Jet View Drive
Rochester, NY 14624

Written by Paul Comon
Editor: Mimi Netzel
Production Coordinator: Marti Saltzman
Layout and Design: Buch & Grafik Design, Güther Herdin
Printed in Germany by Kösel GmbH, Kempten

ISBN1-883403-11-1

Contents

Introduction 10

Using the N6000/N6006

Elementary Operation 12
Mounting the Lens 12
Removing the Lens 12
Installing the Battery 13
Testing the Battery 13
DX Coding 16
Film Loading 16
Controls for Simple Operation 19
Autofocus with the N6006 20
Focusing the N6000 20
Basic Flash Photography with the N6006 21
Film Rewinding and Unloading 22
Tips for Foolproof Operation 23
Most Important, Enjoy Your Camera 26

Exposure Control 27
Exposure Modes 27
Setting the Exposure Mode 28
Lens Requirements 28
Using the Program Mode 29
Using the Multi-Program Mode 30
Flexible Program 32
Using Shutter Priority Mode 33
    Troubleshooting 34
    Choosing a Shutter Speed 35
Using Aperture Priority Mode 39
    Troubleshooting 41
    Stepless Exposure Settings 41
Using Manual Exposure Mode 42
How Meters Work 43
Using a Gray Card 44

Exposure Metering Modes 45
Evaluating Your Results 49

Advanced Functions 51
Controls and Settings 51
Setting the ISO 51
Focus and the Autofocus System 51
Depth of Field 51
Using Depth of Field to Advantage 53
Autofocus with the N6006 54
Tips for Using Autofocus 57
Manual Focus with the N6006 59
Focusing the N6000 60
Tips on Manual Focusing 61
Using the Self-Timer 63
The "Bulb" Setting 65
Automatic Bracketing 67
Setting the Auto Bracketing Function 67
Auto Bracketing with Flash 69
Using Exposure Compensation 70
Motor Drive Modes 71

Using the N8008s

N8008s Camera Controls 72
The On/Off Switch 73
LCD Display 76
Film Loading 76
The ISO Setting 76
Film Advance 77
Film Rewind 77
Multiple Exposure 78
Resetting the Camera 79
Metering Modes 79
Self-timer 79
Power Consumption 80
Battery Status 80
Viewfinder Displays 80
Viewfinder Image 81
Depth of Field Preview 82

Advanced Functions 84
The Autofocus Revolution 84
Autofocus Mechanics 84
The Coreless Motor 87
The Critical Element in the Formula 87
Using Autofocus 89
Single Servo Autofocus 89
Continuous Servo Autofocus 92
Autofocus Viewfinder Information 94
When Not to Use Autofocus 95
Autofocus in Low Light 96
Manual Focus Mode 96
Additional Autofocus Assist 98
The N8008s Metering Systems 99
Matrix Metering 99
Center-Weighted Metering 100
Spot Metering 100
What the Meter is Saying 101
Overriding the Meter 101
Flash Metering 102
Auto Exposure Modes 102
Program Exposure Modes 103
Flash Photography with Program Modes 105
Shutter Priority Exposure Mode 105
Aperture Priority Exposure Mode 106
Auto Exposure Lock 107
Additional Overrides 108
Manual Mode 109

Nikon N6000, N6006, N8008s

Nikon Flash Photography 112
Basic Principles 112
Light Output, Duration and Distance 112
Increased Light and Distance 112
Guide Number 112
Guide Numbers with Zoom Flash Heads 114
Color Temperature 115
Red-eye 115
Flash Synchronization 115

Autoflash Modes 116
Flash Output Control 116
Control of Duration by Reflected Light 116
The Test Flash Feature 116
Conventional TTL Autoflash 116
Limitations of Conventional TTL Flash 117
Subjects with Unusual Reflectance 117
Overview of Nikon System Flash Units 119
Using Flash with the N6000 Series 119
The Built-in Flash 119
General Flash Data 119
Non-Nikon Flash Units 122
TTL Flash Mode 122
Camera Exposure Modes with TTL Flash 122
Manual Exposure Mode 125
Slow Sync 125
Creating Motion Blurs 126
Rear Curtain Sync 126
Matrix Balanced Fill Flash 127
Center Weighted Fill Flash 127
Spot Fill Flash 128
Using Automatic Balanced Fill Flash 128
Using the N8008s with Flash 128
Operating the N8008s with the SB-25 Flash 130
Program Modes with Flash 132
Matrix Balanced Fill Flash 132
Manual Flash Operation 134
Rear Curtain Sync 134
Nikon Accessory Cords and Adapters 134
Non-Nikon Flash Units 136
Additional Information 136

Nikkor Lenses 137
An Overview of Nikon Lens Technology 137
The Metal Bayonet Mount 137
Optimization for Close-up and Long Range 137
Chromatic Aberration and ED Lenses 138
Spherical Aberration and Aspherical Elements 138
Internal Focusing 138
Variable f/stop Design 139

Brief History of Nikon Lenses ... 139
Non-AI Nikkors ... 139
AI Lenses ... 140
AI-S Lenses ... 140
AI-P Lenses ... 140
AF Nikkor Lenses ... 140
AF-D Nikkors ... 144
AF-I Nikkor Lenses with AF Motor ... 144
Lens/Camera Compatibility ... 144
Nikon Camera and Lens Compatibility ... 144
A Tour of Nikkor Lenses ... 146
Lens Characteristics ... 146
Fisheye Lenses ... 147
Ultra Wide-Angle Lenses ... 147
Wide-Angle Lenses ... 148
Normal Lenses ... 149
Short Telephoto Lenses ... 150
Telephoto Lenses ... 150
Super Telephoto Lenses ... 151
Zoom Lenses ... 151
Macro Lenses ... 152
PC Lenses ... 153
Non-Nikkor Lenses ... 154
Teleconverters ... 154
Macro Accessories ... 155
Extension Tubes ... 155
Close-up Filters ... 155

Accessories ... 156
Focusing Screens for N8008s ... 156
Eye Cups ... 156
Eyepiece Correction Lenses ... 156
Cable Releases ... 157
Lens Hoods ... 157
Filters ... 158

Introduction

This book covers three different cameras, two models in the N6000-series and the N8008s. The N6006 and the F-601 are identical cameras. N6006 is simply the designation of the camera sold in the USA, the F-601 is sold in other parts of the world. The N6000 and F-601m are also identical; N6000 is the US version. There are several functional differences between the N6006/F-601 and the N6000/F-601m. The N6006/F-601 offers autofocus, a built-in flash, and a spot meter; the N6000/F-601m does not. The N8008s is the designation for the camera sold in the USA, F-801s is the world version; the F-801 being the same as the N8008. The N8008 is the predecessor to the N8008s. Differences, including an added spot meter and improved autofocus system, are pointed out in the text where applicable. For identical operating procedures, only the N8008s is refered to for the sake of simplicity. However, this book could be applied to either.

The book discusses the operation of the N6000-series and the N8008s cameras separately. The first chapter on the N6000 and N6006 explains in understandable terms, how to set the camera's functions to do most of the work for the user. Only those controls needed for simple use in average picture-taking situations will be explained in this portion of the book. Succeeding chapters will deal with the various advanced functions of the cameras and a brief explanation of the fundamental photographic principles involved. The reader can, in this way, become familiar with as much or as little of the camera as s/he deems necessary.

The N8008 portion is laid out a little differently. As most users of the N8008s are advanced amateurs or professionals, functions, use and photographic theory are all explained together as they pertain to a given feature. The reader can, in this way, understand how technology and photographic skills can be combined for the greatest benefit.

Camera manufacturers continue to add additional features to each new camera model, but very few photographers use every feature contained in today's electronic cameras. People discover that they use some features and functions on their cameras often and may never use others. Remember, a camera is a tool; it is your friend. You should never feel intimidated by it and you should never feel guilty because you do not use and understand every application.

This book will serve as an instruction book and more. Not only will it explain how the cameras work, it will also detail the reasons why the various functions are included, when they are needed and the basic photographic principles involved. It is not essential that the photographer knows every aspect of the art to produce great pictures; but if a person understands some of the theory of photography, the end result, the picture, will be less of a surprise.

With all this in mind, the first section of this book should be read with care. All the knobs, dials, buttons, levers, switches and controls will be identified. The camera operation, in its simplest form, will be explained, and the user will learn how to ensure that unwanted functions are not engaged.

Subsequent chapters may then be carefully read or skimmed, as the reader chooses. Needs change as time passes, and the way a camera is used today is not necessarily the way it will be used at a later date. This is especially true of the photographer whose first good camera is a Nikon SLR (**S**ingle **L**ens **R**eflex). That person should operate the camera using automatic features until confidence is developed, then experiment with additional features, one at a time. A few rolls of film should prove how easy it is to photograph with the N6006-series or N8008s camera, and by then the camera will be more familiar. During this time, a "man and machine" rapport should start to develop. This book can be referred to again and again during this learning period as the photographer increases his/her knowledge of the camera.

Note: *Throughout the text, left and right are used to identify the positioning of various buttons, symbols, etc. on the cameras. These terms refer to the camera when it is held in the shooting position.*

Elementary Operation

The Nikon N6000-series cameras are multi-purpose cameras. They can operate as "point & shoot" cameras or they can be sophisticated and complex. The photographer has the option of making the system as simple or involved as she or he chooses. This chapter will explain using the N6000 and N6006 in their simplest mode of operation. To use the N6006 as a "point-and-shoot" camera, an AF (autofocus) lens is required. The N6000 is almost as simple to use, but the lens must be focused manually.

Mounting the Lens

Several types of lenses may be used on both the N6006 and the N6000. Lenses designated AF or AI are the safest and most compatible with either camera. Attaching older style lenses to the N6006 and the N6000, may do expensive damage to the camera body. These lenses should be avoided until the designations and lens functions are understood. See the chapter, Nikkor Lenses for a more detailed explanation.

Remove the camera body cap and the rear lens cap. Align the lens-mounting index on the camera body (white dot at 2 o'clock on mounting flange) with the aperture index mark on the lens barrel (a white line on autofocus lenses). Seat the lens on the lens mounting flange on the body evenly, keeping it flat with the flange, turn the lens in a counterclockwise direction until it clicks into the locked position. Do not press the lens release button when installing a lens.

Removing the Lens

Push the lens release button and turn the lens in a clockwise direction until the lens will turn no further. The lens can now be drawn away from the body. This should be done carefully maintaining a parallel relationship between the mounting flange and lens until lens clears the body completely. When a lens is not in use, keep lens caps on both ends.

Installing the Battery

Open the battery compartment door by sliding the release in the direction indicated. Insert a 6-volt lithium battery (Mallory DL223A, Panasonic CR-P2 or equivalent) into the chamber, observing the polarity marks on the battery and inserting as indicated on the compartment's inside cover. The battery compartment door will come off if pressure is applied. This safety feature prevents it from being broken. If the door becomes detached, simply insert the tabs into the corresponding slots with firm but gentle pressure until the door clicks into place.

Care should be taken to seat the battery fully. Just below the door-cover seat is a ledge that holds the battery in place. Insert the battery into its chamber and push down so that it exerts just enough pressure on the springs at the compartment base to allow you to slip the battery under the ledge. If a battery is not manually seated under the retaining ledge before the door is closed, the camera will function, but battery life may be reduced by 50% or more.

Testing the Battery

Turn the camera power switch to ON to activate the liquid crystal display (LCD). If the aperture and shutter-speed values remain visible (for eight seconds in the N6006 and sixteen seconds in the N6000), the battery power is sufficient. Do not depress the shutter-release button when checking battery power. Regardless of battery condition, the indicators turn off approximately two seconds after the shutter is tripped and your finger is removed from the shutter-release button.

The battery should be replaced if any of the following occur: the indicators stay visible for less than eight seconds (N6006) after the switch is turned on, the film advances noticeably slower than normal, all indicators on the LCD blink when the shutter release button is slightly depressed, or the shutter will not trip.

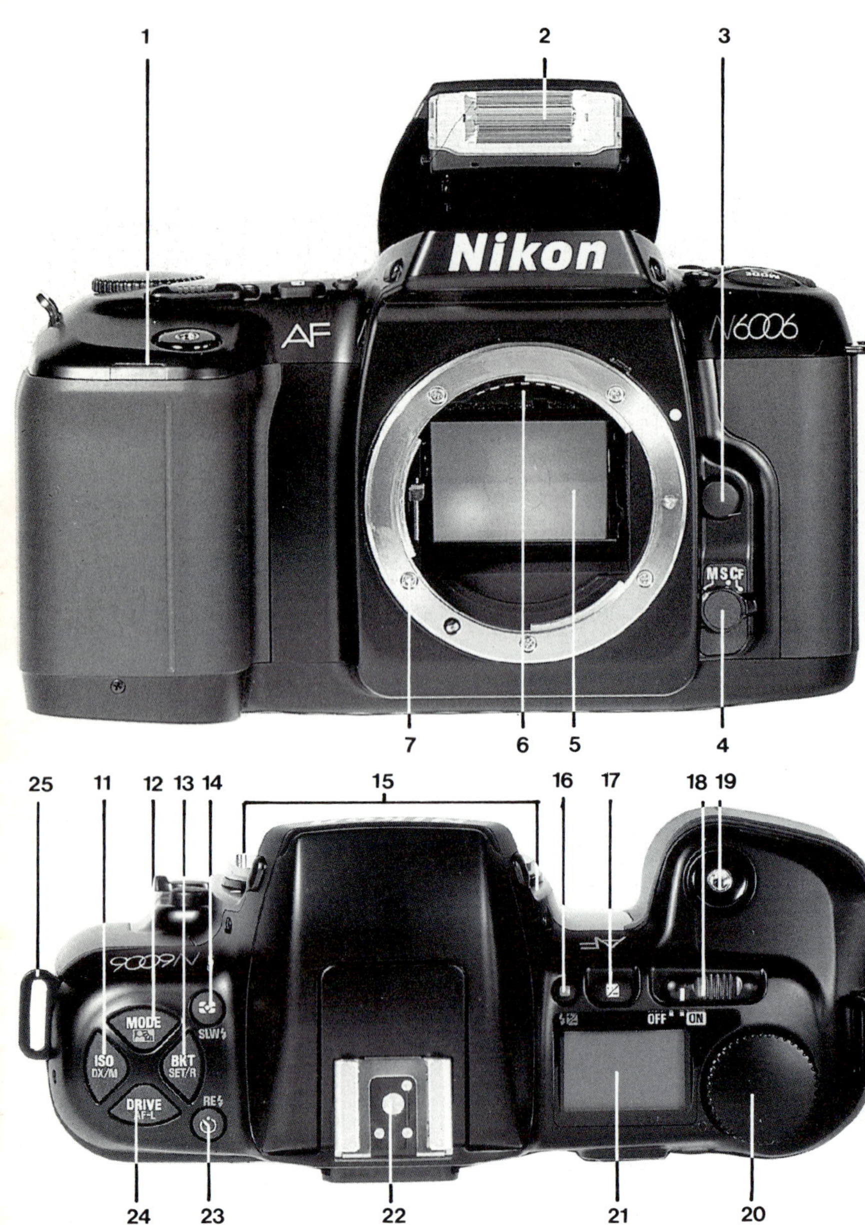
1
2
3
Nikon
AF
N6006
M S CF
7
6
5
4
25
11
12
13
14
15
16
17
18
19
N6006
MODE
ISO
DX/M
BKT
SET/R
SLW
DRIVE
AF-L
RE
OFF
ON
24
23
22
21
20

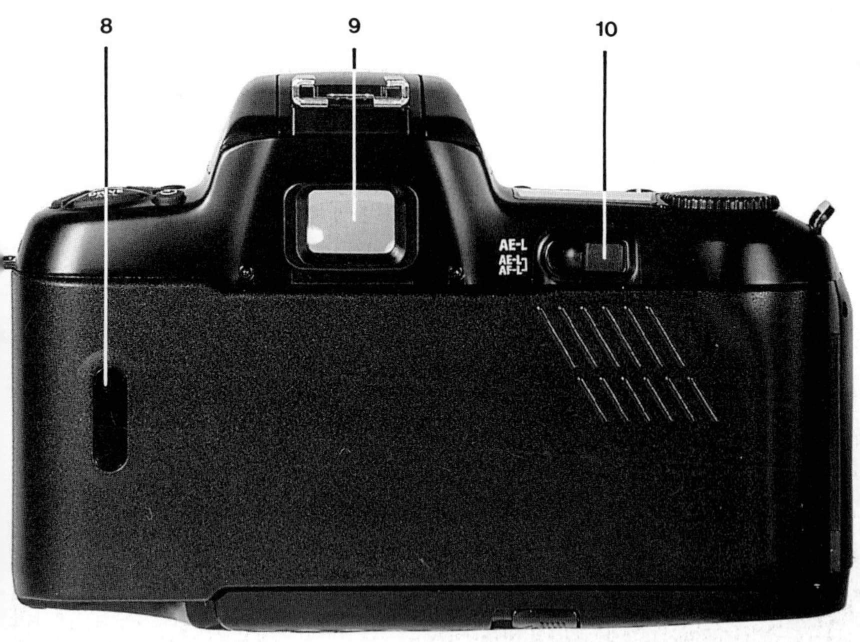

1. Self-timer indicator light
2. Built-in TTL flash
3. Lens release button
4. Focus mode selector
5. Reflex mirror
6. CPU contacts
7. Autofocus coupling
8. Film cassette window
9. Viewfinder
10. Auto exposure lock/autofocus lock lever
11. Film speed setting button
12. Exposure mode/automatic balanced fill flash button
13. Auto bracket button
14. Metering system/slow flash sync button
15. Flash release buttons
16. Shift button
17. Exposure compensation button
18. Power switch
19. Shutter release button
20. Command input control dial
21. LCD panel
22. Hot shoe
23. Self-timer/rear curtain sync button
24. Film advance mode/auto- focus lock function button
25. Camera strap eyelet

The above list charts the progression of a battery that is weak to one with no power at all. Install a new battery when there is any indication that one is needed, because a weak battery can cause poor images.

When the camera is not in use, the power switch should be turned off. The battery should be removed and stored separately if the camera is stored for a long period of time. (Removing the battery will not cause the system to lose memory. A computer chip "remembers" the frame count.) The photographer should try to finish rolls of film in a timely manner so that neither film nor battery deteriorates inside an unused camera.

DX Coding

The N6000-series cameras can set the ISO film speed automatically. To set this function, depress the shift button and the ISO button simultaneously and "DX" will appear on the control panel. DX is the coding found on a majority of film cassettes manufactured today. Sensors inside the N6000-series cameras read this coding and automatically set the film speed.

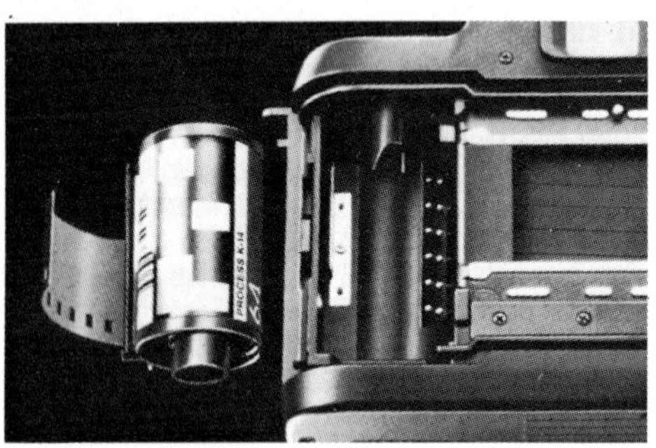

The six sensors which read the DX coding (the "checkerboard" pattern) on the film cassette are visible here on the right side of the camera's film cassette chamber.

Film Loading

Take the utmost care not to damage the shutter blades used in the loading of film in the Nikon N6000-series cameras. These blades are paper-thin metal and if properly cared for will give years of service, but they can be easily damaged. Do not allow anything to touch the shutter blades. Film ends, fingers or even a direct

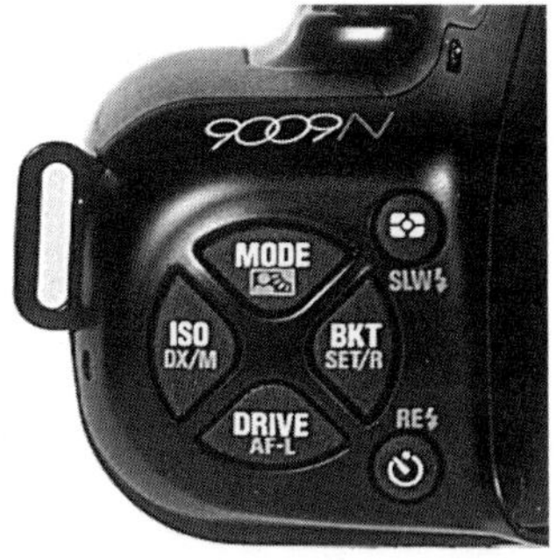

Simultaneously pushing any two of the buttons marked MODE, DRIVE, ISO, and BKT will set the camera for simple fully-automatic operation.

blast from canned air will often cause damage resulting in expensive replacement of the entire curtain. Keep this in mind when opening the camera back.

Push down on the camera back release located on the left side of the camera. The back will then spring open by itself. As you are looking into the open camera back, insert the film in the cavity on the left side of the body. Be sure that the film cassette is seated firmly in place. Pull out enough film leader to extend to the red index mark on the right side of the camera. Check the film to ensure that there is no slack in the leader. Improper leader length may result in misloading. If this occurs, the camera will warn the user of the error and even lock the shutter so that pictures cannot be taken. The film leader should run parallel to the film guides in the camera body. Close the camera back making certain it clicks to indicate it is securely locked. Now press the shutter release button and the film will automatically advance to frame number one. The frame counter on the LCD will confirm this by indicating "1" in the frame counter brackets of the control panel.

If there is a roll of film in the camera, the film symbol will be visible in the LCD, and the frame counter will indicate the frame number, if the film is correctly loaded. The film cassette is also visible in the window in the camera back. If the film is incorrectly loaded, the film symbol and the letters "Err" will blink and the frame counter will display the letter E. If this occurs, simply open the camera back and reposition the film.

Once the camera is properly loaded, the photographer should confirm that the proper ISO is set. To check the ISO any time the camera is loaded, merely press the ISO button and the set ISO will appear on the LCD panel. Match this reading to the information

N6006 LCD Panel

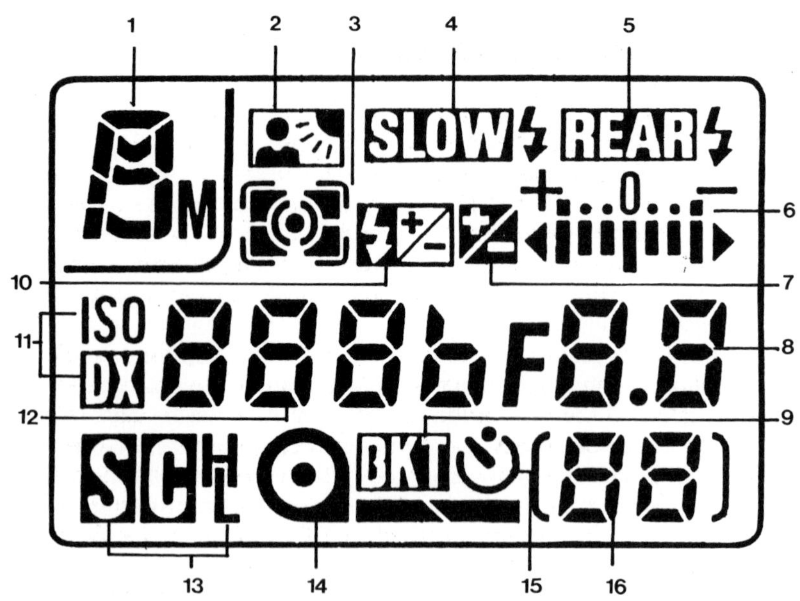

1. Camera exposure mode
2. Automatic balanced fill flash
3. Metering method
4. Slow flash synchronization
5. Rear flash synchronization
6. Analog exposure display
7. Exposure compensation
8. Aperture/exposure compensation
9. Automatic bracketing
10. Flash compensation
11. ISO setting method
12. Shutter speed/ISO/AF-L/# of frames for auto bracketing
13. Film advance mode
14. Film loading, advance and rewind
15. Self-timer
16. Frame counter/frames for auto bracketing/self-timer countdown

on the film cassette seen through the window in the camera back. The number of exposures the roll contains is also visible here.

Controls for Simple Operation

Push any combination of two of the following buttons: MODE, BKT, DRIVE or ISO. Hold them both down simultaneously for approximately two seconds and the camera will reset to "basic shooting" settings. The LCD display will indicate that the camera is set to the Multi-Program (Pm) mode, the meter to the Matrix metering mode and film advance to "S" or single frame. Check that the DX symbol is displayed and the frame counter is not displaying E.

The N6006 requires an autofocus lens for the simplest possible operation. Set the focus mode to "S" using the focus mode selector located on the face of the camera, near the lens mount. This sets the Single Servo Autofocus mode which prevents the camera from firing until the image centered in the viewfinder is in focus. The N6000 has no focus mode selector. Either autofocus or manual focus lenses may be used, but the user must focus the lens manually.

There are some things to look for on the lens. The aperture must be set to its minimum opening (this is marked in orange on Nikkor AF lenses). Most modern lenses have an aperture-lock

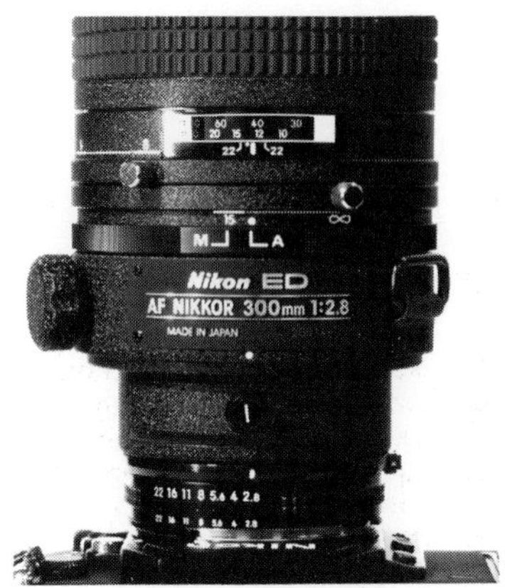

A Nikkor 300mm f/2.8 N ED IF AF showing the M and A settings for manual focus or autofocus.

lever that will prevent accidental movement of the aperture ring. This device is usually located near the widest aperture setting mark. Use this lock to prevent unpleasant surprises.

Some Nikkor AF lenses have an A-M switch, usually located in the vicinity of the distance scale. For autofocus operation (N6006), it should be in the A position, and for manual focusing it should be positioned to M (N6000 or N6006).

Autofocus with the N6006

While looking through the viewfinder, depress the shutter release button. The object you see in the focus brackets will be focused upon by the autofocus system. So if the object of principal interest is not in the center of the viewfinder, reposition the camera so that the brackets encircle the subject. Partially depress the release button until the confirmation circle is visible in the display at the bottom of the viewfinder. Reposition the camera so the composition is to your liking, then depress the button all the way to take the picture. This is how the Single Servo Autofocus mode works.

Focusing the N6000

Look through the viewfinder and choose the object that should be in sharpest focus. Turn the lens focusing ring until the image in the two halves of the split-image rangefinder coincide. A manually-focused camera can be pointed anywhere, focused, repositioned, and the image recomposed without the shutter-release button being partially depressed. Only autofocus cameras require the above focus-lock procedure for off-center subjects.

At times, a split-image rangefinder can present difficulties because there is no vertical subject line to focus upon. When this occurs, it is advisable to locate a line at the same distance and focus on it. Eyes, for example, are difficult to focus upon when using a rangefinder of this type. Good points to focus on include the subject's eyeglasses or a shirt collar. The camera can also be turned vertically to focus on a horizontal line, if that aids focusing. See also, page 20.

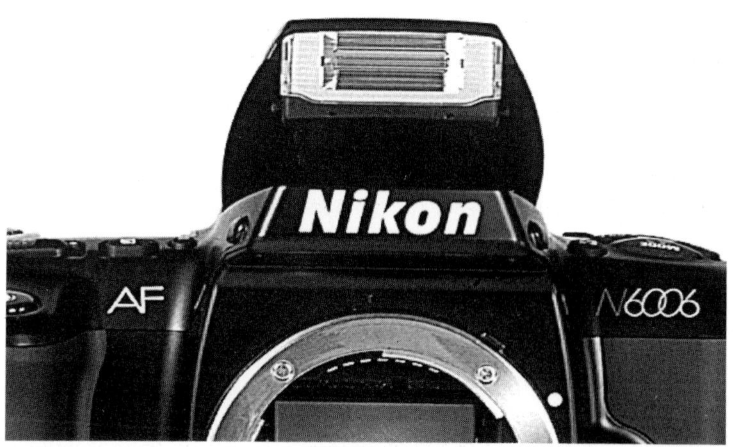

Although not extremely powerful, the handy built-in flash on the N6006 camera works well for fill flash and close subjects.

Basic Flash Photography with the N6006

Using the built-in flash on the N6006 is unbelievably easy. First, raise the flash to its ready position by squeezing the flash release buttons on both sides of the flash head. Next, position the camera, lightly depress the shutter release button and wait for the ready signal to come on. The ready signal is a lightning bolt visible in the display at the bottom of the viewfinder. This indicates the exposure can be made when the photographer wishes.

The built-in flash is only good to distances of approximately eighteen feet with ISO 200 speed film and a normal (50mm) lens set at f/2.8. If greater distance is required, a more sensitive film or supplementary flash is needed. The optimum solution to flash at distances beyond eighteen feet is a larger, supplementary flash.

A supplementary flash unit must be used with the N6000 as it has no built-in unit. Because the cameras offer both automatic and manual flash control options, using flash can be as simple or complex as the photographer feels comfortable with. For a complete description of the options, functions and uses of electronic flash units, refer to the section of this book devoted to flash photography.

Film Rewinding and Unloading

When the last exposure has been made on a roll of film, the N6000-series cameras warn the user and prevent some errors that once plagued photographers. These user-friendly cameras prevent film from being ripped from the cassette and prevent the unsuspecting user from attempting to take forty-seven pictures on a thirty-six exposure roll.

When the roll is fully exposed, the camera will no longer attempt to advance the film. At that point, both the word END and the film cassette symbol will blink on the LCD panel. If the film is not rewound, each time the shutter release button is pressed the letters ERR and the film cassette symbol will blink on the LCD panel.

To activate the motor-driven rewind procedure, slide the film-rewind lever in the direction indicated by the arrow. While holding the lever, press the film-rewind button (both on the base of the camera) to start the rewind process. While the film is returning to the safety of its cassette, the user can observe the frame counter on the LCD counting down until the rewinding procedure is complete. When rewinding is completed, the rewind motor automatically stops, the frame counter shows E and the cassette symbol blinks. Now the camera back may be opened and the film cassette removed.

The same rewind procedure will work, even if all the exposures on a roll of film are not used. Reasons for premature removal of a roll may include the need for a different ISO film, a change from black and white to color, or the desire to switch from slide to print film (or vice versa).

Film rewinding takes a substantial amount of battery power so it is not uncommon for a weak battery to die in the middle of the rewind cycle. If this happens, replace the battery, make sure the power switch is on, then start the rewind procedure again, using the same method as before. Never open the camera back unless the camera is empty, the film is completely rewound or the camera is in total darkness.

The Nikon N6000-series cameras rewind the film leader completely into the film cassette. This prevents the user from loading a roll of film that has already been exposed.

Tips for Foolproof Operation

Exposures should be made with both hands on the camera (unless a tripod is used). Camera movement can ruin a photograph, even at relatively high shutter speeds if the camera is not properly supported. Select a grip that is comfortable, but be sure that it does not interfere with the camera's operation. For example, do not hold the lens in a manner that would interfere with the autofocus mechanism, and do not put your finger(s) in front of the flash.

The shutter release button should be smoothly depressed, not jerked. If the shutter speed indicator blinks (in the viewfinder and on the LCD panel), it is warning you that the selected shutter speed may be too slow to handhold the camera. Blurred pictures may result if precautions are not taken. The simplest solution is to either use flash to take the picture or mount the camera on a tripod.

When the shutter speed indicator blinks and flash photography is inappropriate, one of several solutions may be applied. A tripod is the most positive way to guard against camera movement. For greater mobility than a tripod will afford, a monopod may be the ideal accessory. When the photographer can use neither a tripod nor a monopod, and the shutter speed indicator blinks, there

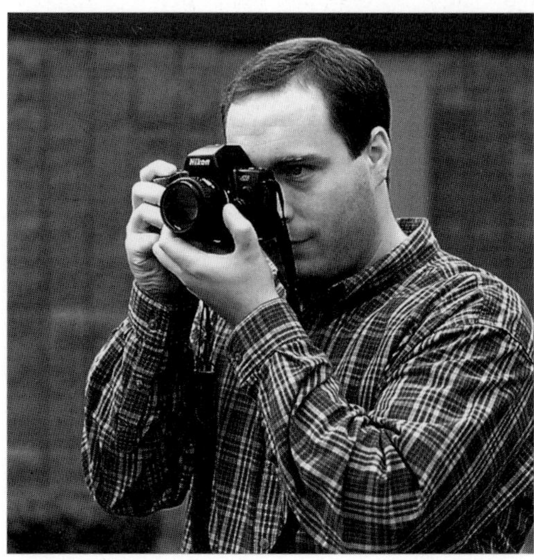

Proper handholding technique is comfortable, supports the camera and does not interfere with camera operation.

is always the possibility that the camera can be supported on a table or other flat surface. No matter how steady the camera is held, if the shutter speed is slow and the subject is moving, motion blur may occur. Slow shutter speeds are recommended only if the subject is still or subject movement is desired.

If handheld pictures are the only possibility, there is still hope. For the steadiest possible handheld pictures, the photographer should assume a wide but comfortable stance, place his elbows against the sides of his rib cage and the camera against his forehead. While in this position he should take a deep breath, let half of it out and squeeze off the shot. The mortality rate on such shots is high, but surprisingly, some do turn out well. Make several shots to increase your chances of getting an acceptable picture. It is better to try and fail than not to try at all.

If the letters "HI" blink (in both displays), the warning means that overexposure may occur. This will probably only happen if high ISO films are used in bright sunlight. The easiest fix for this is to change to a film with a lower ISO. The general rule for choosing film is ISO 100 for sunny days, ISO 200 or 400 for overcast days and for flash photography.

If the letters "LO" replace the shutter speed numerals in the displays, underexposure may occur. This indication warns that the setting required is below the camera meter's ability to compute the exposure correctly. The easiest fix for this would be to use flash or a faster film (higher ISO). When the lightning bolt flashes in the display, the camera is recommending that a flash be used. The camera user should heed the warning and either use a flash or one of the alternate methods described above.

Setting the camera for automatic operation allows the photographer to concentrate on other aspects of photography, such as choosing subjects and composition. ➪

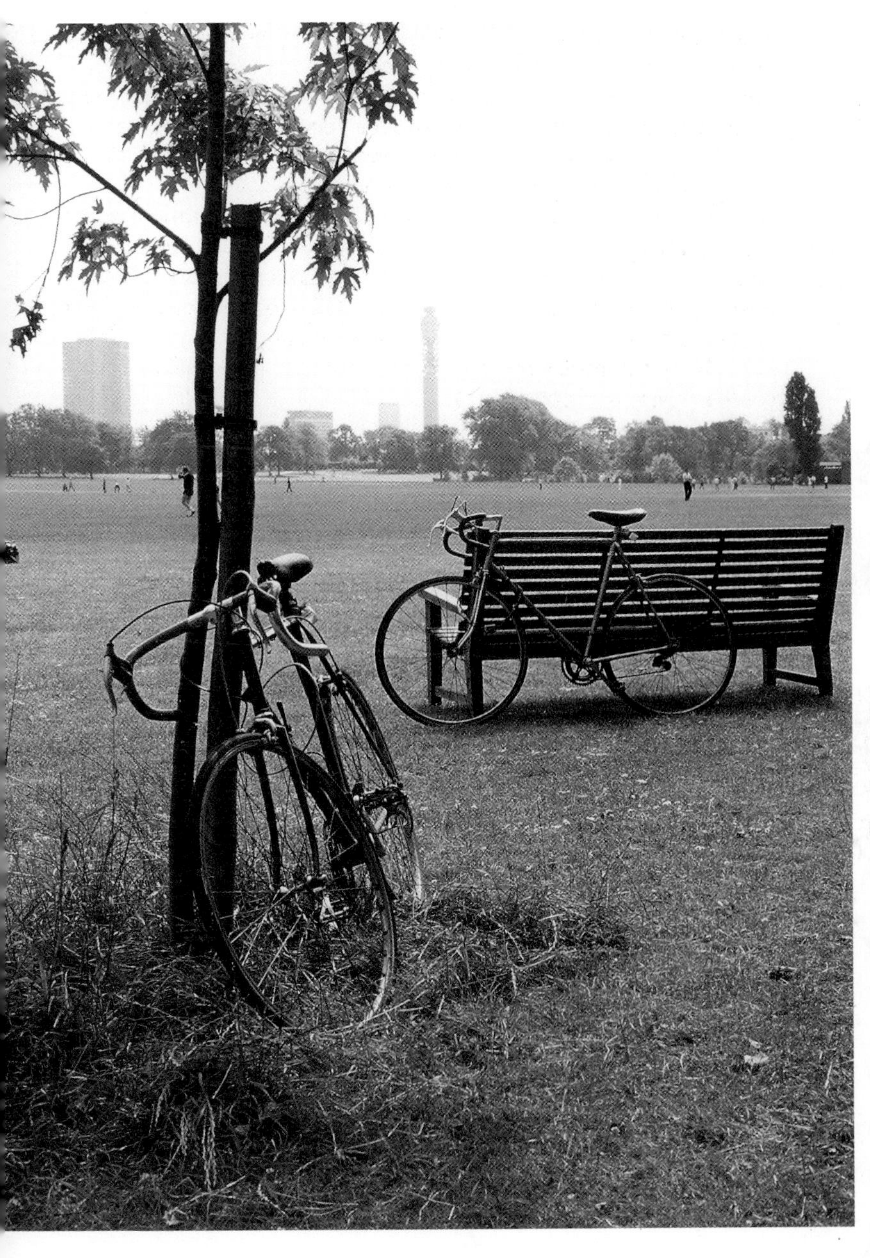

Most Important, Enjoy Your Camera!

These are all the instructions needed to take good pictures with a Nikon N6000-series camera 90% of the time. Remember to watch the displays in the viewfinder and the LCD display on the camera top.

Now is the time to shoot a few rolls of film using only the elementary procedures described in this chapter. Look at the results and share them with someone who can give good advice; your local camera store may be the place to start. When you feel you have a solid understanding of basic camera operation, you are ready to move to the additional functions and features of your Nikon, if you so choose.

The remainder of the camera's features are no more complicated than the procedures you have already learned. To avoid confusion, study one function at a time. Then, after reading about each operation, try making images using each new technique.

Exposure Control

The Nikon N6000-series cameras offer four automatic exposure modes, as well as manual mode. The photographer can have as little or as much control over the factors that govern exposure as he/she would like.

Exposure controls have a balanced relationship. Shutter speed and lens aperture settings work together to control the amount of light needed for correct exposure, while film speed dictates what that amount of light needs to be. How motion is portrayed is dependent upon the shutter speed, but the aperture must be adjusted to compensate for the change in shutter speed, thus affecting depth of field.

Is a high shutter speed important for stopping action? Would using a slow shutter speed to convey motion be more dramatic? Should a small lens aperture be used for greater depth of field? Should a large aperture be used to blur a distracting background? The final parts of this puzzle will come together in this chapter and the photographer will discover how to control these critical decisions.

Exposure Modes

Here is a brief description of the five modes. We will discuss how to set and use each of them, and the strong and weak points of each mode.

Program (P): For normal, bright sun shooting, where a specific shutter speed or lens aperture is not of dire importance, this is the program of choice.

Multi-Program (Pm): In Multi-Program mode, the camera chooses higher shutter speeds, so there is less chance of blur from subject or camera movement.

Shutter Priority (S): In this mode, the photographer chooses the shutter speed, and the camera will select the appropriate lens opening to yield proper exposure.

Aperture Priority (A): Here the photographer chooses the lens aperture and the camera's system selects the shutter speed automatically.

Manual (M): This mode gives the photographer full control over shutter speed and aperture.

Setting the Exposure Mode

Begin by turning the power switch to ON. While pressing the MODE button, rotate the command dial to obtain the desired exposure mode setting. The dial can be turned in either direction. The mode selected will be displayed in the LCD panel and in the viewfinder display, with one exception. The LCD display will differentiate between Program and Multi-Program, the viewfinder display will not. "P" or "Pm" will be displayed in the LCD readout, but in either of these modes, only "P" will be displayed in the viewfinder.

Lens Requirements

In the "P", "Pm" and "S" modes, the camera sets the lens aperture automatically, so the camera and lens need to "communicate" with each other. Therefore, only current lenses with the designa-

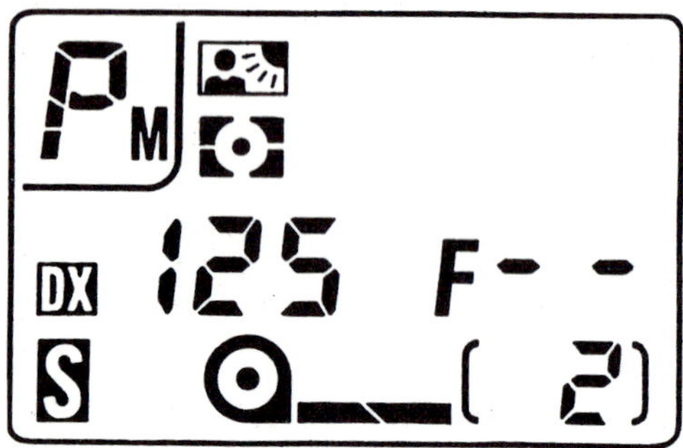

F-- appears on the LCD panel in place of the set aperture if the lens being used cannot be controlled by the camera.

tion AF (autofocus) or AI-P (non-autofocus lenses with built-in CPU's) can be used with these programs on the Nikon N6000 and N6006 cameras.

If a lens is used which cannot be controlled by the camera, "F--" will appear on both displays and the exposure mode will blink. The photographer must use the camera in the aperture-priority mode or the manual mode. The metering system should be set to either centered-weighted or spot metering (N6006 only).

Using the Program Mode

The computer in Nikon N6000-series cameras is designed to process important exposure information for any given shot. The factors considered are: film ISO, brightness of the scene, the lens' focal length and the maximum aperture of the lens. Photographers using the Program mode need only press the shutter release and watch the LCD and viewfinder displays. Blinking symbols on the displays are the camera's way of warning the user there may be a problem.

The Program mode was designed to produce the best results if the image is a typical snapshot, such as scenery or a group portrait. Your traveling companion standing beside the car with some of the Grand Canyon in the background, or the flowers in your garden in full bloom are ideal subjects for the "P" mode, especially with the meter set in the matrix mode.

The Nikon engineers have designed the Program mode of the N6000-series cameras so that in poor light a large lens aperture is used. If the quantity of light increases, the program will increase

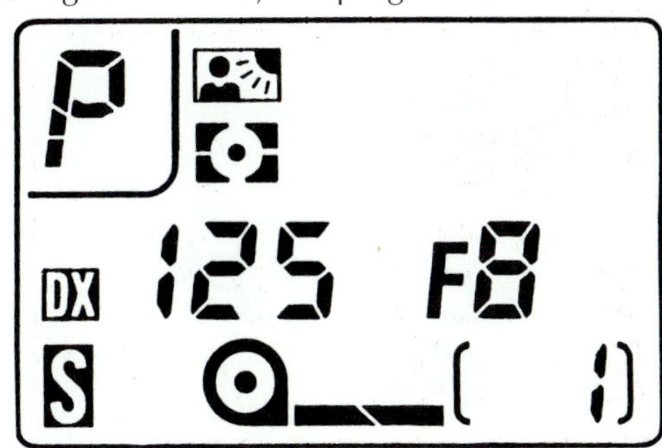

The LCD panel of the N6006 in the Program mode.

the shutter speed, reducing the chance of motion blur. At a point that varies with each lens' focal length and maximum aperture, when the light level is sufficient, the program begins to close down the aperture. Beyond this light level, both aperture and shutter speed are adjusted simultaneously.

To sum up the Program mode, it is the mode that should be used by photographers who are just learning. It is also the ideal mode for use when shooting pictorials, especially scenics in good, strong light. "P" mode is also a good choice when shooting posed people or other slow-moving subjects. In most flash photography, especially automatic flash modes, including TTL (through-the-lens), "P" is an excellent choice of modes. Even when a person becomes more familiar with the N6000-series cameras, "P" is still an excellent mode.

Using the Multi-Program Mode

In the "Pm" mode, the camera's computer reacts to the lens attached. The longer the lens' focal length, the faster the shutter speed the camera will select. This is important because longer, heavier lenses are harder to hold steady and they magnify any movement. Therefore they should be used with faster shutter speeds. In the "Pm" mode, the shutter speed settings are allowed to climb to higher speeds than in the "P" mode.

When the camera is set in the "Pm" mode, "Pm" blinks in the LCD display and "P" flashes in the viewfinder display. In this instance, flashing displays are merely a reminder that the camera

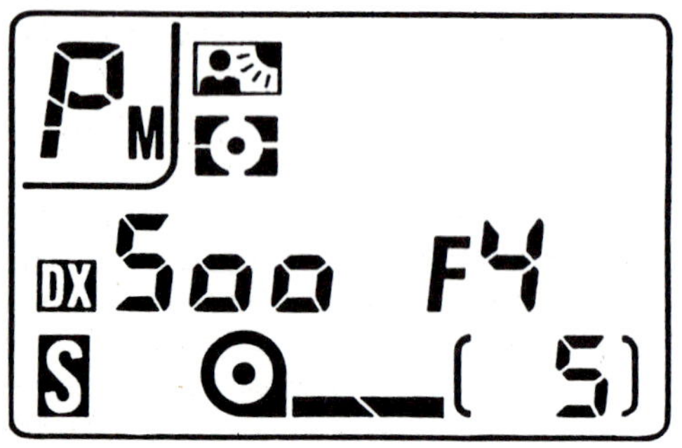

The LCD panel of the N6006 in the Multi-Program mode.

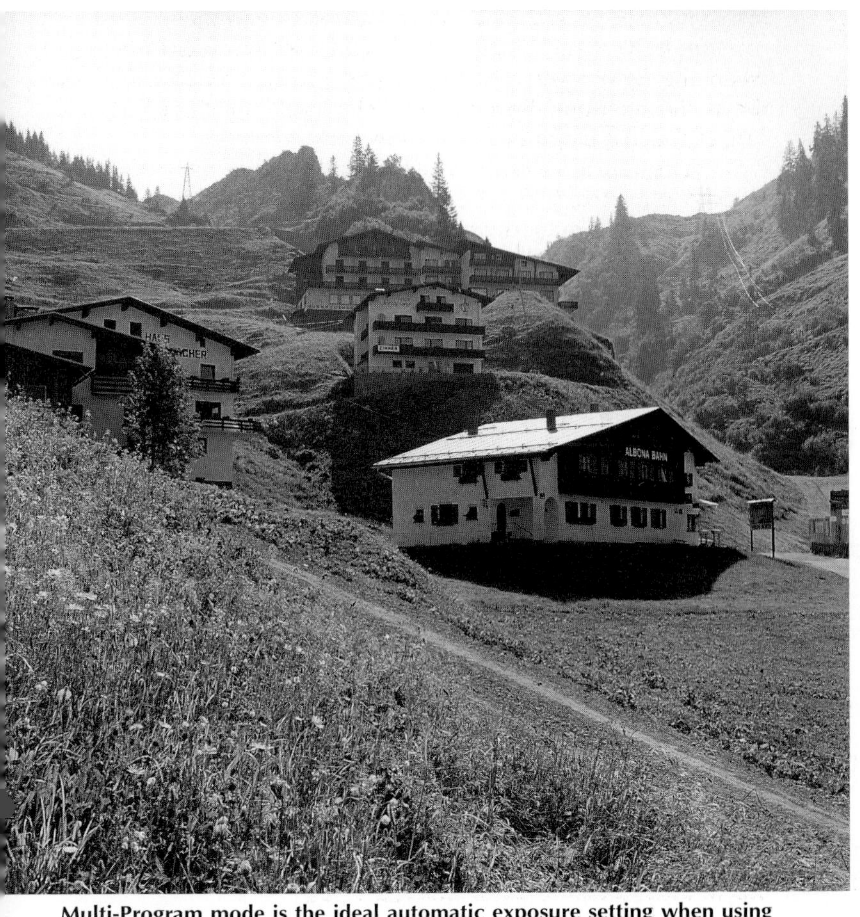

Multi-Program mode is the ideal automatic exposure setting when using a long focal length lens to photograph picturesque scenes.

is in the "Pm" mode (usually flashing displays signal trouble, but not in this case).

The Nikon N6000-series cameras were designed to work well as point-and-shoot cameras, but, incrementally, they can become as controllable as the user desires. Most N6000-series camera users will probably outgrow this mode, but it is a nice learning tool. It will give the novice confidence to graduate to a more sophisticated mode and open up additional possibilities. Use the

"Pm" mode to build confidence, then move on to the next step of camera operation. Also use it when the program mode is satisfactory, but one or two shots (in the series) need more finesse than the straight "P" mode offers.

The benefits of the all-automatic exposure modes are they free the photographer from the mechanics of taking a picture. This allows the photographer to concentrate on things the camera cannot control, like subject and composition. A good photographer should be aware of everything that is going on in the entire scene. The novice usually is so intent on an individual idea that disturbing or disruptive elements in the picture may be ignored. Before shooting, learn to recognize problems that may result in poor images. Is there anything distracting or unwanted in the viewfinder? Is there some action that requires a high shutter speed? Is the camera selecting an f/stop capable of adequate depth of field? Ask yourself these questions, and more, before tripping the shutter release. Detailed notes on f/stop, shutter speed, lens focal length and other technical data, as well as how the image was intended to look, can be a photographer's most valuable learning tool.

Notice that I never use the word amateur. The phrase "amateur photographer" has a bad connotation. It should not. No one should be ashamed of being an amateur. The word is derived from the Latin word "amator" which means lover. Therefore an amateur photographer is one who loves to photograph. The phrase says nothing about the individual's ability or inability. In my dealings with photographers from all walks of life, I can honestly say that I have seen as many excellent photographers in the amateur ranks as in the professional ones.

Flexible Program

In the "Pm" or "P" modes, the camera can be operated in "flexible program". When the camera is set to a program mode, the user simply rotates the command dial, in one direction or the other, until the desired lens aperture or shutter speed appears. When the dial is turned, both aperture and shutter speed move together in increments of one exposure value (EV). Remember, if the exposure value is to remain constant, you cannot move the shutter speed without a lens aperture compensation or vice versa.

As soon as the viewfinder and LCD displays disappear, the "flexible program" is automatically canceled and the next time the camera is activated it will be in the prior mode. This will happen if the N6006 shutter release button is not pressed in eight seconds, or if the main switch is turned to OFF. This is also true of the N6000, but its display will remain active for sixteen seconds.

Using Shutter Priority Mode

This is an extremely useful mode, when mastered. The camera is still controlling the overall exposure determination, but the photographer can govern the action-stopping ability of the camera. The Nikon N6000-series cameras will automatically select the correct aperture for proper exposure as you select the shutter speed, provided AF or AI-P designated lenses are used. Set the camera to the "S" mode as described earlier in this chapter. Now all you need to do is rotate the command dial until the desired shutter speed appears in either display. Before attempting to use this mode, be sure the aperture setting on the lens is at its smallest opening. Most modern lenses have a lock to prevent the aperture setting from accidentally being moved out of position. It is advisable to lock the lens aperture whenever the mode ("P", "Pm", or "S") calls for the lens to be set to its smallest aperture.

To operate in the "S" mode, after the lens aperture is locked and the shutter speed is selected, look in the viewfinder and lightly depress the shutter release button. Check the aperture chosen by the camera, keeping in mind the effect of the aperture on a

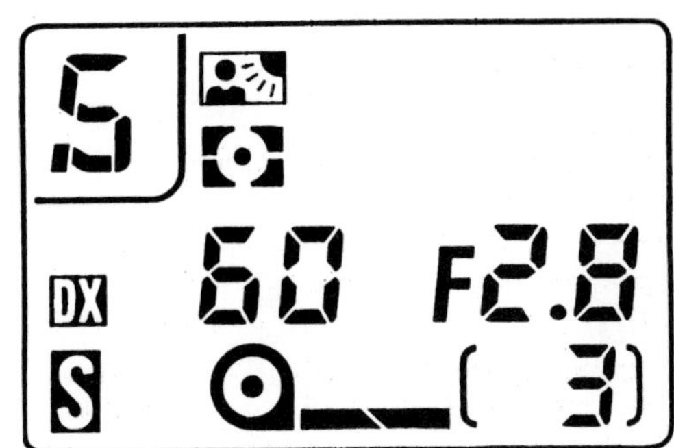

The LCD panel of the N6006 in the Shutter Priority mode.

photograph. If the aperture is satisfactory for the image, depress the release button to make the exposure.

Troubleshooting

If "HI" appears on the displays, it is warning that the photograph will be overexposed if no correction is made. A higher shutter speed, slower film (lower ISO) or neutral density filter are all possible solutions.

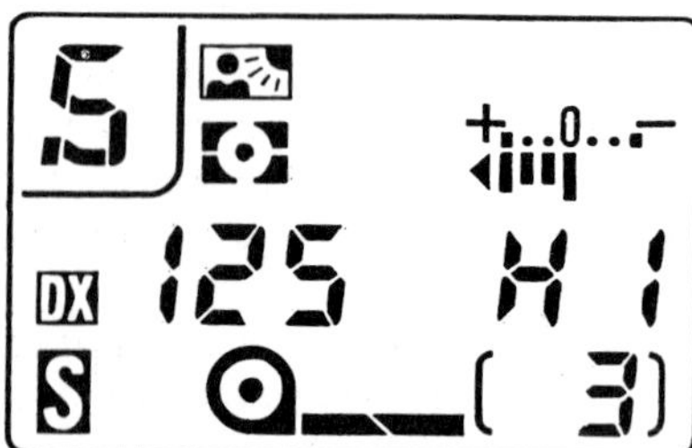

The blinking "HI" indication is an overexposure warning. Choose a higher shutter speed, smaller aperture or use a neutral density filter.

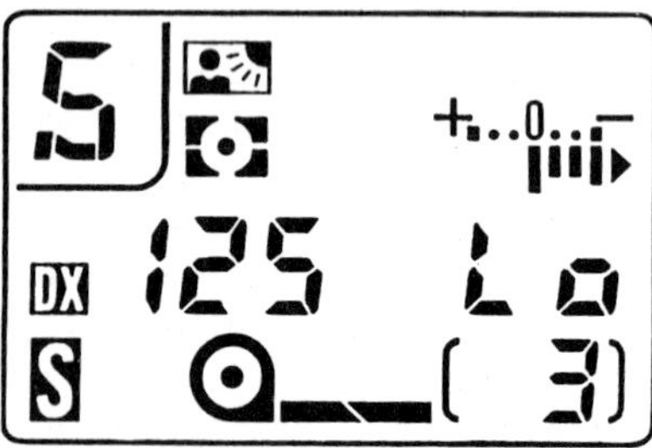

The blinking "Lo" warning indicates underexposure. You should select a slower shutter speed or use flash.

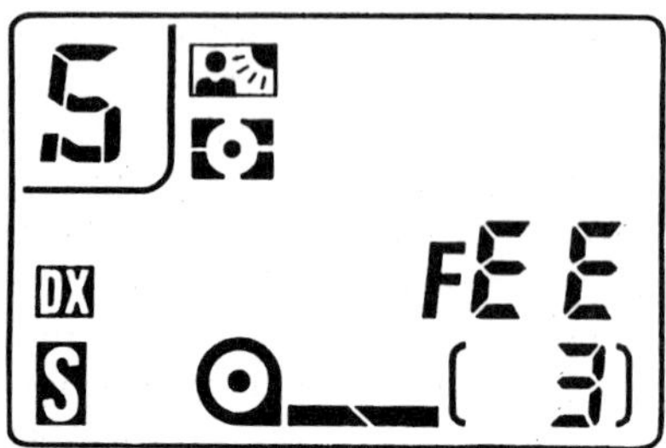

The blinking "FEE" warning indicates a lens setting error. Check that the lens is set to the smallest aperture (largest f/stop number).

If "LO" blinks on the displays, underexposure is probable. Try a slower shutter speed, faster film speed (higher ISO) or an electronic flash to solve the problem.

If "FEE" blinks, the lens has not been set to its smallest aperture. The shutter release will not trip if the aperture is not set properly. The remedy to this problem is to stop down the lens aperture and lock it.

Choosing a Shutter Speed

A brief overview is in order on how the shutter speed effects an image. As a general rule, most people can handhold a camera with a normal (50mm) lens at a shutter speed of 1/60 second or faster. Longer focal length lenses require higher shutter speeds. The rule of thumb is that the shutter speed should be the reciprocal of the focal length. Simply stated, a 60mm lens or shorter, can be handheld at 1/60 second, while a 500mm lens would require a shutter speed of at least 1/500 second.

Still subjects can safely be photographed at 1/60 second, 1/125 second will usually stop a person who is walking, and it is usually safe to shoot a human runner at 1/250. At 1/500 second, all but the hooves of a running horse will probably be frozen. Race cars may also be stopped at this shutter speed, but 1/1000 second is a better shutter speed choice for this type of event.

All of these are generalizations however, there are many variables. If action is approaching the camera on a perpendicular axis, a high shutter speed is needed to stop the action. If action is approaching the camera obliquely, a slower shutter speed will suffice. Objects that approach the camera head-on can be stopped with an even slower shutter speed.

Not all human beings are equally steady. Not all cameras are equal in terms of shutter and mirror bounce. Wind, the surface on which the photographer is standing and countless other factors influence steadiness. Rather than pondering the situation, photographers should experiment with their equipment. Learn the requirement of each camera body/lens combination by trial and error. Also, bear in mind that on some days you will not be as steady as on others. However, there are tips that will allow you to handhold the camera at slower shutter speeds than the unknowledgeable snapshooter. Any contact with a solid, unmoving object will help. Leaning backwards against a tree or a solid wall is bet-

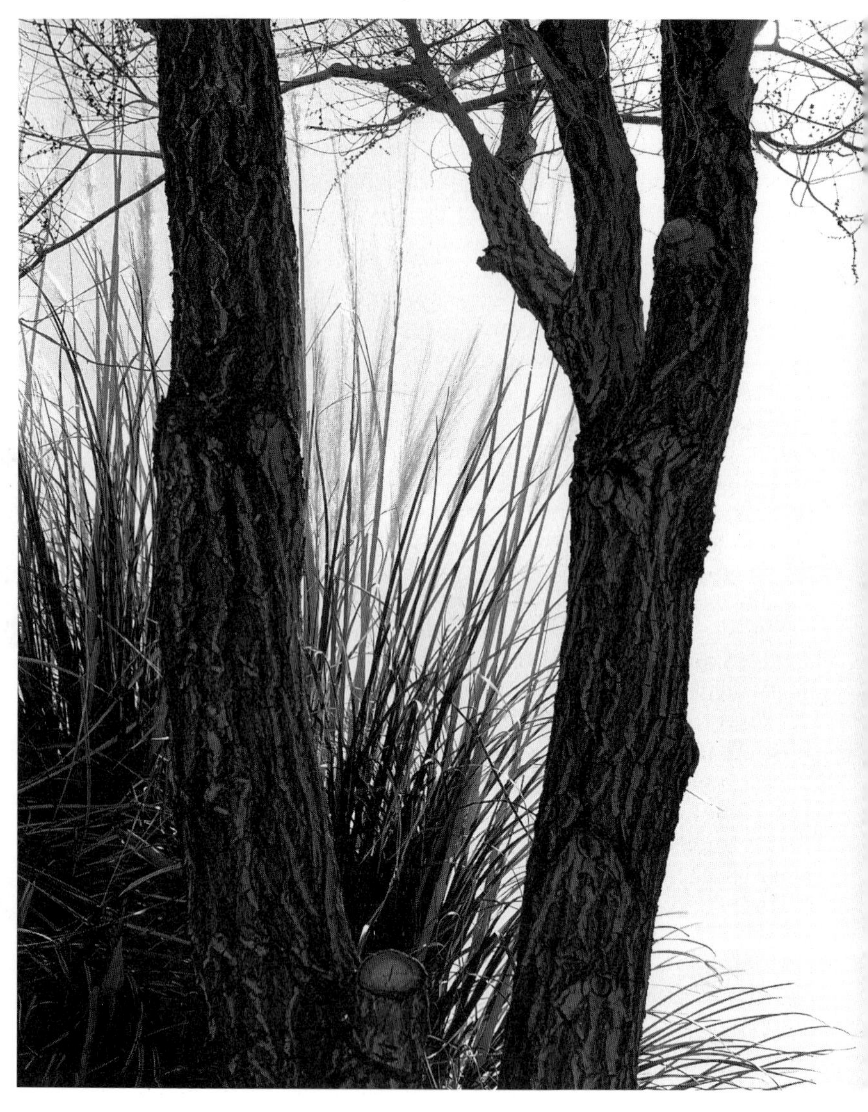

The reeds in this picture were moving violently, but a 1/500 second shutter speed makes them appear still.

ter than tripping a slow shutter while standing in the middle of a floor. If you are going to take the picture standing, start by taking a wide stance; not uncomfortably wide but wider than normal. One foot should be slightly ahead of the other. The toe of the trailing foot should be as forward as the instep of the other foot. Tuck your elbows into your rib cage and rest the camera against your forehead to give it support. Finally, take a deep breath, hold it for a second then let it half out. Now, squeeze the shutter release button.

When shooting at slow shutter speeds, even better results can be obtained if the camera is rested on a solid object such as a tripod. A monopod is helpful, and much more portable, but a tripod is more stable. The rule about tripods is to use the biggest one that you will take with you. Two examples of bad tripods follow: one is so flimsy that the camera it is supposed to support quivers in a slight breeze, or worse, topples when barely bumped. The other is so heavy that it spends its entire life in the closet. Longer telephoto lenses require heavier tripods, therefore photographers should consider buying a tripod large enough to support the longest lens they intend to buy.

When thinking about shutter speeds, consider this guide: faster shutter speeds generally produce sharper images, slower speeds are often used for creativity. But the only way to really understand what happens when you manipulate the shutter speed is to experiment. Try photographing running water, such as a waterfall, a fast-moving stream, waves pounding the shore or some other water movement. Observe the results of shots taken at 1 second, 1/15 second, 1/60 second and 1/250 second. Another technique to try is called "panning". It uses slower shutter speeds to stop fast moving objects. Panning means following the action with the camera, so the position of the moving object in the viewfinder remains approximately the same. If done properly, the moving object is relatively sharp but the background is rendered as a complete blur. Panning requires some practice to choose the correct shutter speed for the subject. In general, use shutter speeds from 1/8 to 1/30 second with slower subjects requiring slower shutter speeds.

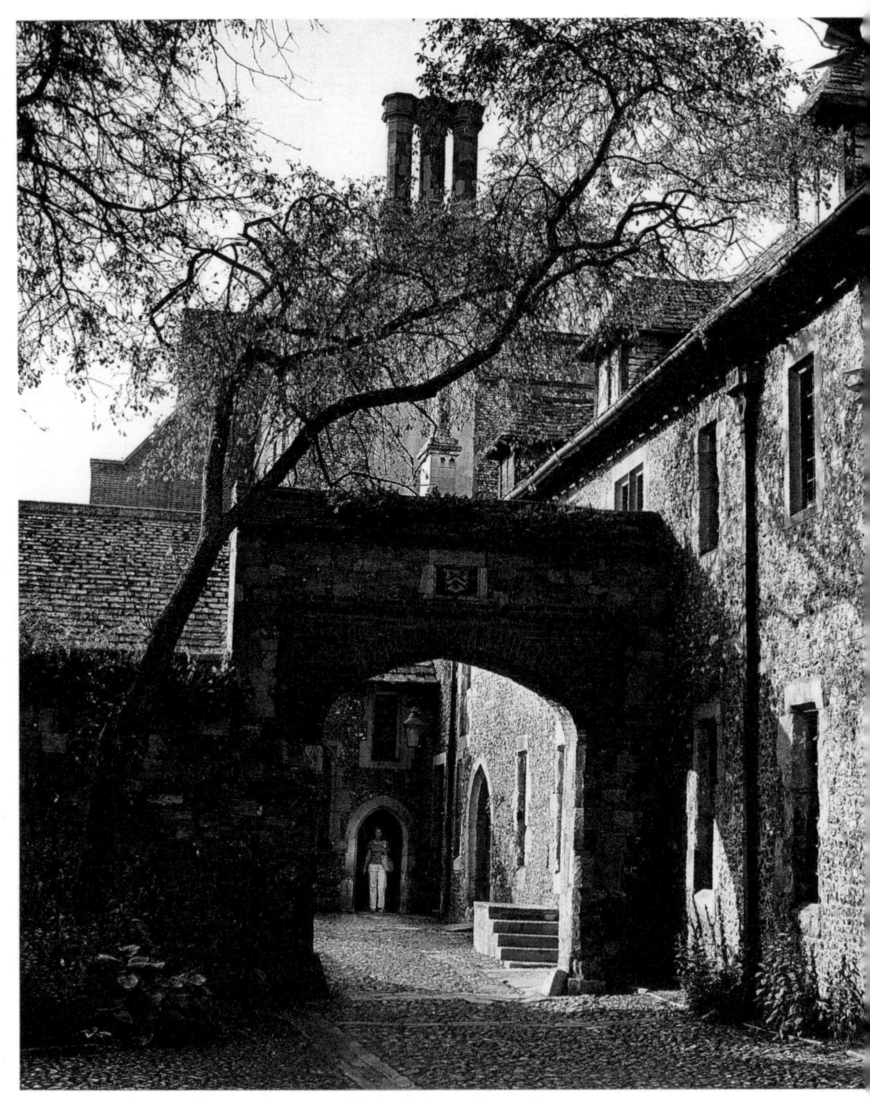

For greater depth of field in this shot of Winchester College in England, the lens was stopped down to f/11 and the arch, which is approximately 1/3 of the way into the scene, was the point of focus.

Using Aperture Priority Mode

This mode, as the name implies, lets the camera user control the aperture setting while the camera's CPU sets the correct exposure by adjusting the shutter speed. Virtually all lenses perform best when the aperture is stopped down to approximately its mid-point. When used wide-open or stopped down to its minimum settings, the same lens will produce softer results than when set in its middle range. Most lenses for 35mm cameras produce the sharpest results when used somewhere in the f/5.6 to f/11 range. Even though depth of field increases at smaller settings, maximum sharpness at the point of focus will occur with settings somewhere near f/8.

Some photographers prefer the "A" setting over any other automatic mode. This mode offers control over the lens setting, but because of the reciprocal relationship between aperture and shutter speed, the shutter can also be controlled. The "A" mode allows the photographer to use the aperture ring when he really wants to change the shutter speed. When looking through the viewfinder, it is easier to turn the aperture ring than the shutter speed dial. Because the N6000-series cameras have full-information viewfinders, this is a quick, efficient way to work. Try moving one and then the other without removing your eye from the viewfinder, and decide which is the fastest and most comfortable for you.

To use the camera in the aperture priority mode, set the camera using the method described above via the mode button plus the command dial. Next, set the lens to the desired f/stop. If the aperture ring has a locking device it must be released before the

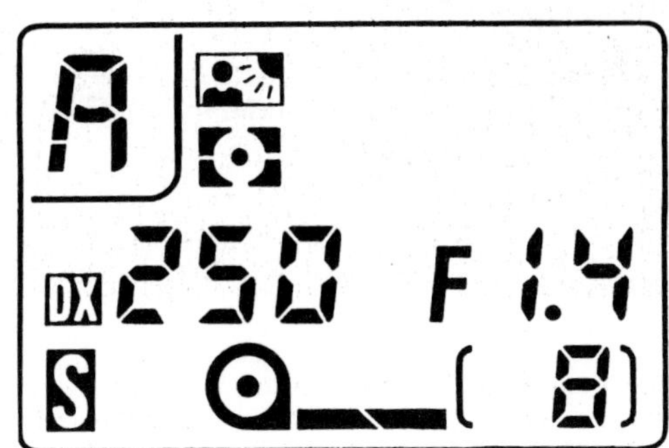

The LCD panel of the N6006 in the Aperture Priority mode.

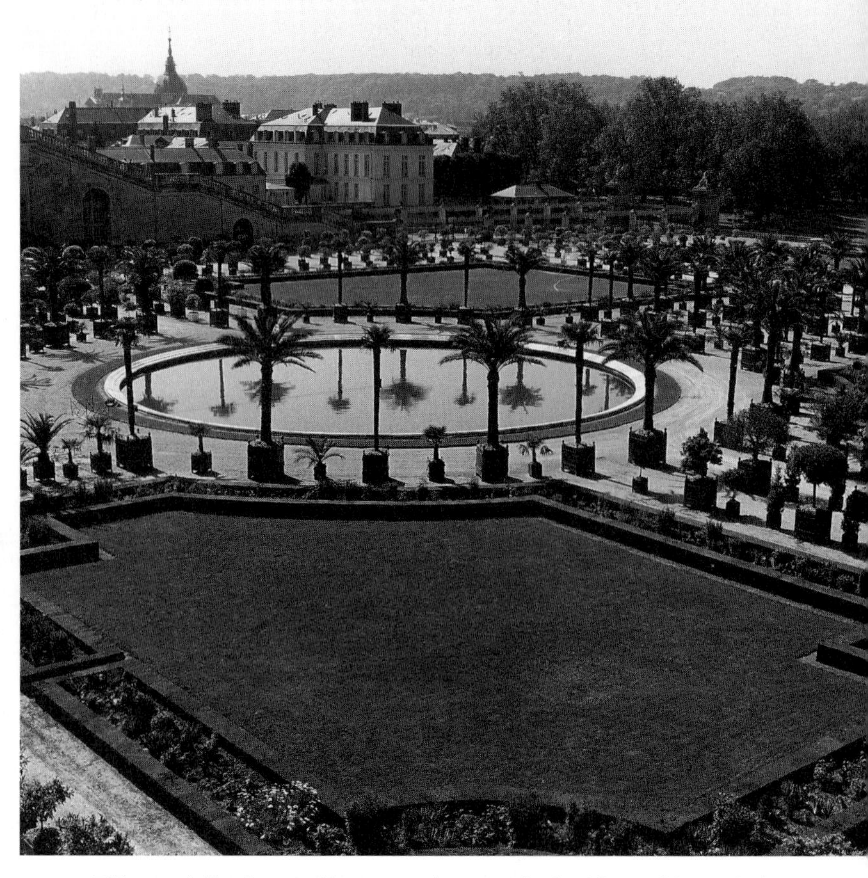

This spacially deep subject was photographed with a wide angle lens. The photo's great depth of field was achieved by using a small aperture opening selected in aperture priority automatic mode.

aperture ring can be turned. When the aperture is turned, the user can watch the settings change in the viewfinder. The right index finger is used to depress the shutter release button while the left hand rotates the aperture ring. Additional steadiness can be obtained if the left palm is under the camera body while the left

With the camera in Manual mode, the LCD displays an analog meter scale. Here the meter is indicating that at the set aperture and shutter speed, the image would be overexposed by 1/3 stop.

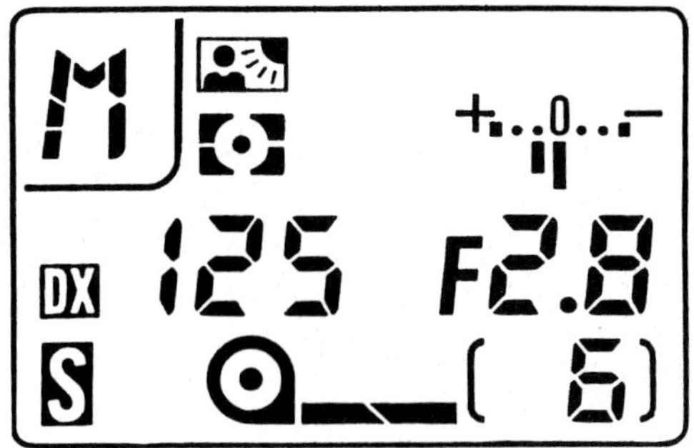

index finger and thumb cradle the lens-setting ring. The photographer need only select the aperture, confirm that the shutter speed will produce the desired effect, and then trip the shutter.

Troubleshooting

These warnings will appear in both displays to signal possible trouble. The shutter speed blinks at speeds too slow to handhold, "HI" appears when overexposure is imminent and "LO" blinks if the image will be underexposed. The symbol "F--" will appear if a lens containing no CPU is used on an N6000 or N6006. This does not mean the lens cannot be used though. The system will perform properly, but the displays will not supply the f/stop information. If the camera user needs aperture information, he must obtain it by looking at the lens itself.

Stepless Exposure Settings

In all four of the auto exposure modes, stepless shutter speeds and/or apertures are selected that are not available in manual mode. Stepless means that shutter speed or aperture settings are not limited to the conventional numbers which appear on the LCD and in the viewfinder. Shutter speeds, such as 1/24, 1/158 to 1/584 or apertures of f/4.6, f/5.7 or f/8.9, may be chosen to maximize exposure within the exposure range of the film. In the "PM", "P" and "S" modes, the aperture selected by the camera can be any fraction though the camera will only inform the user of those numbers. In the "PM", "P" and "A" modes, the shutter speed is stepless and again only those shutter speeds which are commonly known will be displayed.

Using Manual Exposure Mode

This mode implies that the photographer must pair-up the aperture and shutter speed that will yield correct exposure. In a way this is true, but the light meter will guide the photographer by displaying what the correct exposure should be. In this mode, spot readings may be taken, gray cards may be read and interpretive settings made.

Manual is the most creative mode, and it should be considered as the exposure mode of choice when serious lighting problems are encountered. If the problem can be solved by using a flash, or some other form of light, that should also be considered. But when all else fails, a manual reading (or better yet, several manual readings) are in order. If meter readings are taken to determine the brightest and darkest areas of the scene the photographer knows what the boundaries are. Then if a mid-tone reading is taken, experience will come to the rescue.

The only way to learn this system is to use it. The first attempts may not be stellar, but future problems of a like type will be easier to master. If the person learning photography thinks things over before reacting, the learning process will be shortened.

Using the manual mode is really quite simple. If the aperture locking device is engaged, unlock it. Next set the exposure mode to "M" by rotating the command dial while depressing the mode button. At this point, when the displays are activated an analog scale is displayed. Exposure can be controlled by rotating either the shutter speed dial or lens aperture ring. Correct exposure is achieved when only the single bar under the "0" is visible. This scale can be used to determine up to one EV of over- or underexposure, in 1/3 stop increments. If the reading is off by more than one EV, an arrowhead appears on either the plus or minus side. The arrowhead only appears on the side where the exposure deficiency lies.

In the manual mode there are no safeguards, no warnings, no blinking displays; you are on your own. The only display warning that may occur is the "F--" that appears when lenses that contain no CPU are used. Again, this will not cause problems, other than the lack of display information regarding aperture.

One very safe way to learn how to use manual exposure is, after taking a picture, in any mode you are comfortable with, set the camera to manual and read the exposure in the "M" mode. Does that reading compare with the reading obtained in the mode you actually used? If not, can you figure out why they differ? You may want to expose another frame and compare the results.

Some photographers may never venture into the M mode. It certainly is not essential for good photography. But good photographers should know their craft, and manual exposure is one element that can change craft to art.

How Meters Work

Before studying the exposure metering systems in the Nikon 6000 series cameras, some basic metering fundamentals should be understood. Exposure meters are designed to yield a correct rendition of an object that is middle or 18% gray. All meters, handheld, built-in, automatic or manual work on this principle. The N6000 series cameras use a TTL or Through-the-Lens meter design which measures only the light coming through the lens. The sensitivity of the meter is determined by setting the ISO speed of the film in the camera. When the meter is activated, it reads the brightness of the scene and calculates exposure for the subject, assumed by the meter to be middle gray. This is because manufacturers know that in the vast majority of cases, photographs are taken of a scene or a subject of so-called average brightness. An average black and white, bright sunlight scene, if all the tones were mixed, would produce this 18% gray tone. Thus, meters choose exposure settings as though every subject were "average" or 18% gray.

To illustrate this, consider a situation in which a meter reading is taken of a gray card, a white card, and a black card. The card must fill the viewfinder or spot metering circle for an accurate reading. All three meter readings will be different because each subject is reflecting a different amount of light. Nevertheless, all three pictures will look like photos of a gray card. Because when the meter "saw" a gray card, it gave the correct readings for the exact average between black and white or middle gray. For the white card, the result was underexposure causing it to look to dark and with the black card, an overexposure because, in both cases, the meter is designed to "believe" all subjects are gray.

These guidelines should be carried out within the framework of identifying your subject and basing your metering decisions on that subject. This becomes especially critical in situations in which the light on the subject is different than the light in the rest of the scene. Common examples of this include a subject which is backlit by a sunrise or a window, or a person standing in the shade of a tree on a sunny day. Obviously, it is most important that the subject be correctly exposed, however a meter reading of the entire scene will average the bright sunlight into the exposure causing the subject to be underexposed.

Using a Gray Card

For truly accurate exposures, many photographers take light readings off of an 18% gray object in the scene. Typically they use a gray card, available through photographic retailers. It does not matter what type of light meter you are using or what mode your camera is in, a properly used gray card will tell you what normal exposure should be.

The card may be held in the hand or rested on any object. The only two things that matter are: the card must face the same position, relative to the light, that the subject does, and the meter reading must be of only the gray card and nothing else. If the camera is in the spot-metering mode, the camera need not be as close to the gray card as a camera set in either the matrix or center-weighted mode. When using either of the latter modes, be sure that not even the slightest sliver of background can be seen in the viewfinder. Focus is not important. Regardless of the mode employed, be sure you are not casting a shadow on the card. The 18% gray card must be lit in the same manner as the scene.

Using a lightmeter is simple. Ten percent of the lighting situations cause ninety-five percent of the problems. If you understand what has been said here about exposure, you know more than most photographers using sophisticated cameras today. Have confidence!

Exposure Metering Modes

Let us now consider how the above information relates to metering via the Nikon N6000 series cameras. The N6000-series cameras offer several metering options for different situations. Matrix metering is recommended for all but the most difficult lighting situations, such as backlighting.

Matrix metering: The image is metered in five sections. Exposure is then calculated by the camera's computer based on the total amount of light measured and the contrast difference between each section. Matrix metering can be used in any of the exposure modes. It can also be used for flash-exposure control with any properly dedicated TTL flash unit.

Left: Matrix

Center: Center-weighted

Right: Spot

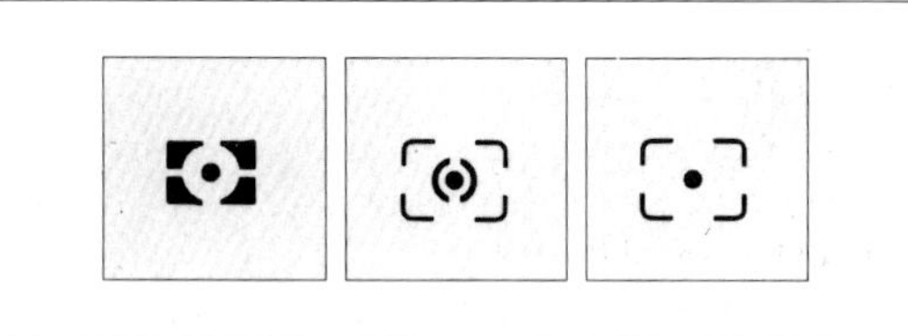

Matrix metering is the optimum mode for the majority of subjects and the least likely to be confused. The system has been programmed to cope with reflections, glare, heavy shadows and all the phenomena that caused earlier systems to produce erratic results. It will provide consistantly accurate exposure readings except in extreme lighting situations. Matrix metering is only possible with AF and AI-P lenses. If the lens in use is not so equipped, the matrix symbol blinks and the meter automatically reverts to the center-weighted mode.

Center-weighted metering: The image is metered in two sections. The center metering zone contributes 75% of the data used to calculate exposure. The area surrounding the center circle provides the additional 25% of the information. Although it does not have the technological sophistication of matrix metering, under some conditions it will do a better job.

Use center-weighted metering on backlit subjects. If the backlit subject covers a large portion of the viewfinder, and you wish to

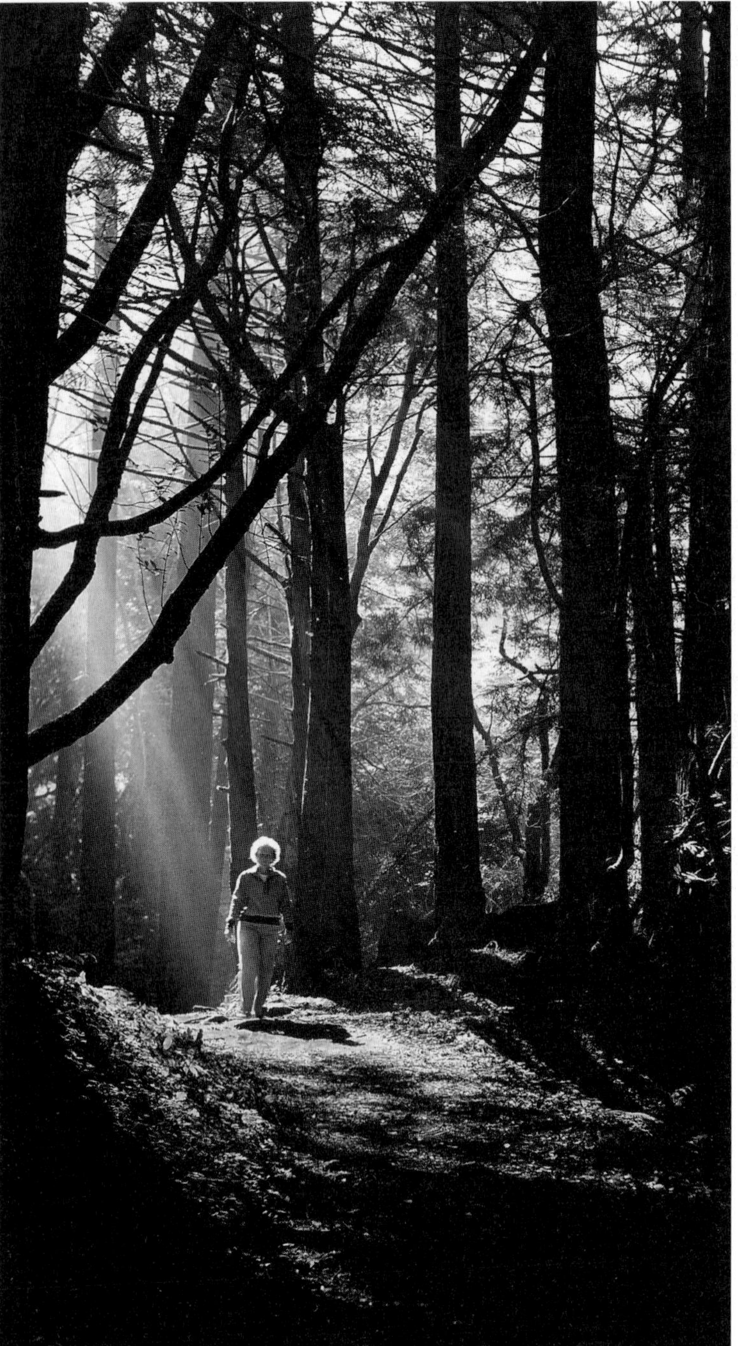

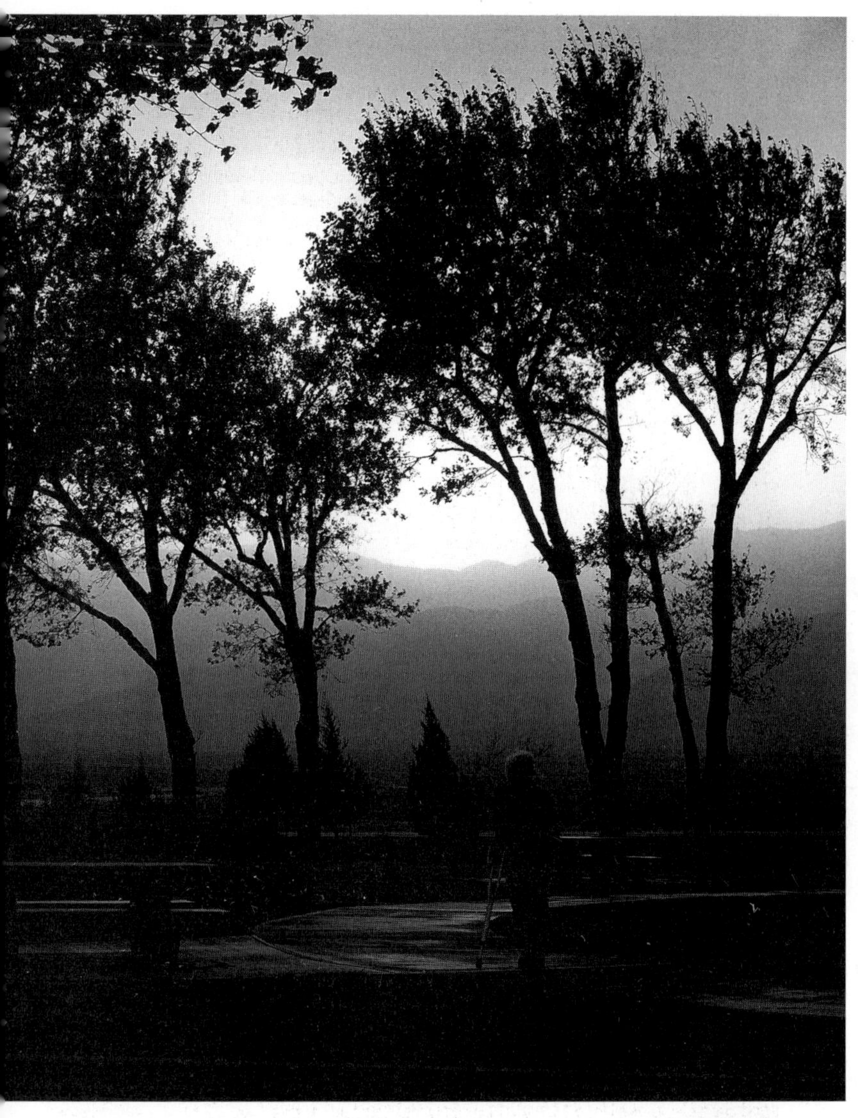

Above: Spot metering in manual mode was used to get a good exposure of this photo taken at dusk in the High Sierras. However, center-weighted metering mode would probably have worked just as well.

⇦ Center-weighted metering resulted in a perfect exposure of this high-contrast shot taken amongst the California redwoods.

expose primarily for the subject while still retaining some detail in the surrounding scene, center-weighted metering is in order. Use center-weighted metering when photographing a small dark subject against a bright background. If the subject is not in the center of the finder, use center-weighted metering in conjunction with the auto exposure lock.

Use center-weighted metering when photographing sunsets. This metering mode will probably produce the dramatic sunset effects desired without any special care, correction or fancy calculations. Unusual scenes, or conditions, require back-up shots. Even the most experienced photographer should shoot several variations if the scene has great potential.

Spot metering: Offered only by the N6006, spot metering should be reserved for those in the know. Exposure is calculated from a light reading taken off of a very small portion of the subject. The area covered by the spot meter, in the N6006, is represented by the 3.5mm circle in the center of the viewfinder. Its prime advantage is that the photographer can see exactly what is being metered. In this mode, there are no surprises, no factory generated biases, just accurate, precise measurement of the light being reflected off of the subject.

Remember, all meters read the subject or scene as being 18% gray; spot meters are no exception. The user of a spot meter, built-in or handheld, must be prepared to interpret the meter reading for good results. Spot metering is usually used in the Manual exposure mode or with Auto Exposure Lock. Rarely is the subject so centered in the viewfinder as to make spot metering possible without metering and then recomposing.

Setting a metering mode: First, make sure that the main switch is turned to ON. Then, while depressing the Metering System button located on the top left side of the camera, rotate the Command Input Control dial until the desired symbol appears on the LCD panel.

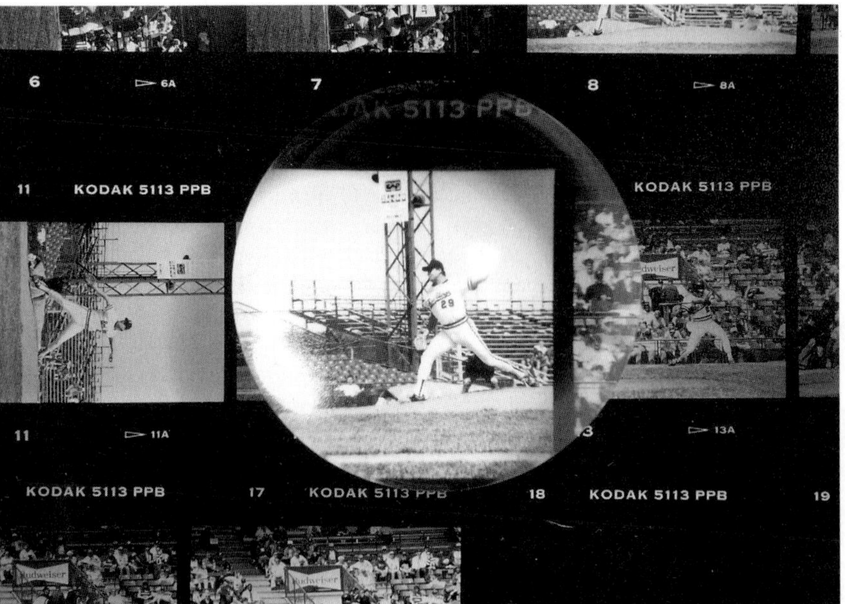

A magnifier, such as the LGL Light Gathering Loupe from Saunders, can make it easier to examine and evaluate negatives, photographs, and contact sheets.

Evaluating Your Results

Film is the least expensive commodity in photography. For learning purposes, a high quality film and a good lab are a must. Most photographers choose color negative film. It is the easiest film to have processed and printed. Prints are the most convenient way for people to view and display photographic images.

Slide film, sometimes called transparency or chrome film, produces a single positive image of each exposure and is preferred by some photographers. Pictures taken on slide film are usually meant to be viewed with a slide projector or used in magazines, on posters, etc. If a great image is recorded on slide film, a print can be made also, but prints from slides are more expensive than prints from negatives. If the photographer wants only one print from each 36 exposure roll of slides, that is less expensive than 36 prints from a 36 exposure roll of negative film.

Comparing the results may not be as easy as it first appears. Most people today do not develop and print their own work. If you do not, a lab that is trustworthy is absolutely necessary. Also, if you are not sure how to read processing results, you need a person whom you can trust behind the photofinishing counter. If you are shooting black and white or color prints, and the results are not what you expect, the lab may be at fault. A knowledgeable photofinisher should be able to offer some insight into what went wrong or at least rule out lab error as the cause.

Most novices are unfamiliar with all the problems that can occur. There are a number of factors that must come together to produce a good photograph. Problems that look indescribable to a novice may be easily recognized by an experienced photographer. Excellent ways to meet other photographers include joining a camera club or taking a photography class. If you have any questions (there are no dumb questions), ask for help.

Advanced Functions

Controls and Settings

The Nikon N6000-series cameras are equipped with additional functions which have one thing in common, they are not as widely used as the simple functions. If you are just learning how to work your new camera, these settings are good to know about, but the elementary functions should be mastered first. This section explains the camera's more advanced features and function so that you can use them when the need arises.

Setting the ISO

As described on page 16 in the section "DX Coding", the N6000-series cameras can set the film speed automatically. Film speed can also be set manually by the photographer to any standard film speed within a range from 6 to 6400. This is preferred by photographers who do not want to use the manufacturers film speed rating. For example, underexposing slide film slightly by setting a lower ISO yields more saturated colors.

Focus and the Autofocus System

Focusing a camera can be a simple task which is obviously made easier thanks to autofocus. But whether you focus a lens manually or let the camera focus itself, a few principles should be understood. While they are simple and straightforward, the photographer who understands them will get better results than the one who does not.

Depth of Field

This term refers to the area, in any photograph, that is in sharp focus. It is really not a complex concept and understanding how it works is equally simple. When a lens is focused on a point,

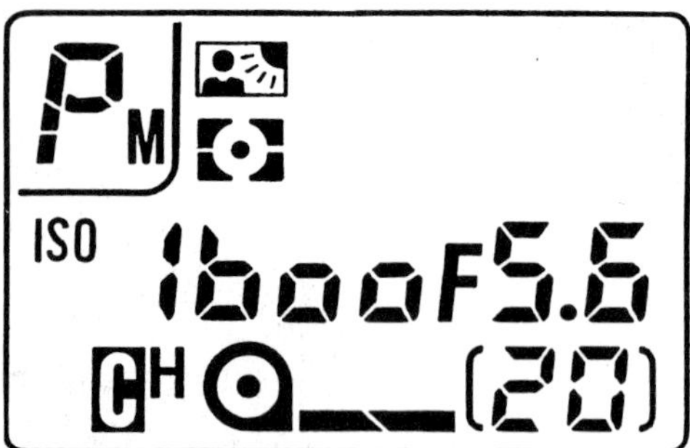

The LCD panel of the N6006 with the ISO set manually to 1600.

depth of field distributes itself in this manner: one-third in front of the focus point and two-thirds behind. Because of this, a person who wants the maximum range of sharpness in a picture shouldn't focus on infinity. This is because a lens focused on infinity is only utilizing one-third of its depth of field capability (the third in front of infinity). Instead, the lens should be focused one-third of the way between the close object and infinity.

Take full advantage of the depth of field range at any given aperture by using the lens' depth of field scale. To utilize a depth of field scale note the effective aperture opening in use. Set the infinity mark on the focus scale opposite this aperture designation on the right side of the depth of field scale. Now find the identical aperture designation on the left side of the depth of field scale. The distance on the focus scale which is opposite that designation will be the closest distance which will be in focus at that aperture.

Depth of field can be used in reverse to soften unwanted backgrounds. Two influencing factors within the photographers control are lens aperture and focal length. If a lens is used wide open (smallest aperture number) it has the smallest possible depth of field. When stopped down to the smallest opening, depth of field is at its greatest. A wide-angle lens has more depth of field than a normal or telephoto lens. The wider the lens' angle of coverage the greater its depth of field.

Many photographic operations are interlinked. Focus, depth of field, lens aperture, lens focal length, shutter speed and even film speed (ISO) all affect one another. Just remember that when the lens aperture is closed down, depth of field increases. A short focal length lens yields more depth of field than a telephoto does

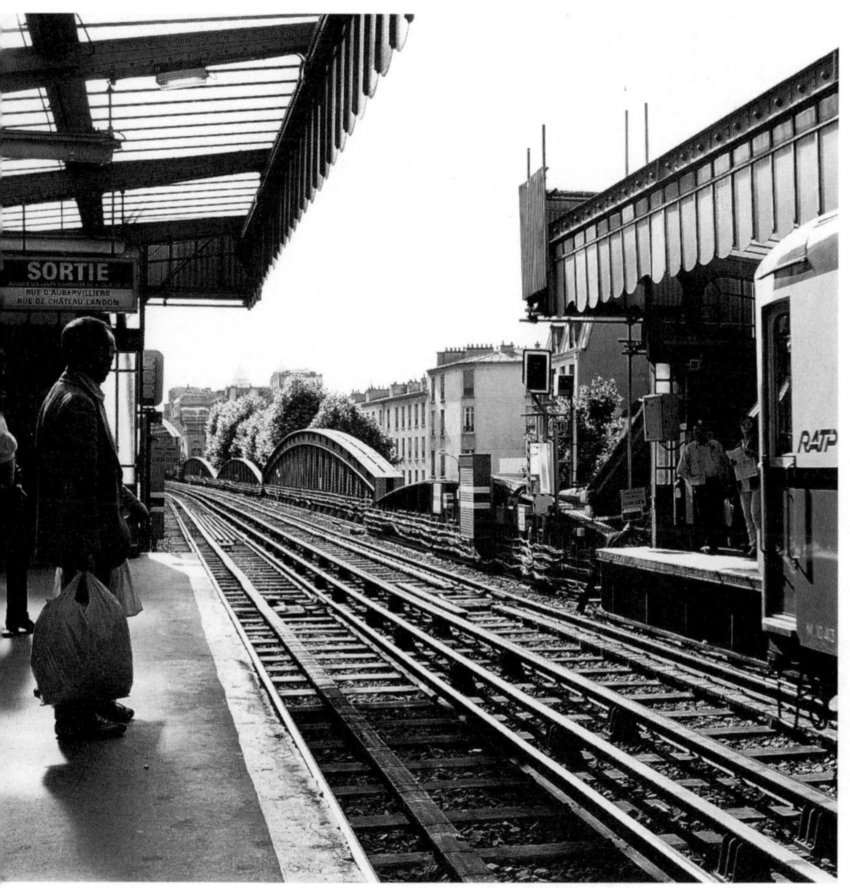

The extreme depth of field in this picture places equal emphasis on the people waiting on the platform and the empty train tracks to convey a feeling of anticipation.

and depth of field takes place in thirds: one-third in front of the point of principal focus and two-thirds behind it.

Using Depth of Field to Advantage

The area in sharp focus, in any picture, can be determined before the exposure is made. Most fixed focal length lenses (both Nikon and other brands) have a depth of field scale on their barrel. Zoom lenses generally do not because there are too many variables.

To locate the depth of field scale, find the line that indicates the focus point. If there are smaller lines (with f/stop numbers) on either side of the focus indicator, these lines indicate depth of field. If the exposure calls for f/8, the range on the lens distance scale that falls between the two lines marked f/8 will be in focus.

When both infinity and close objects need to be sharp, the solution is to place infinity (on the lens focusing scale) opposite the appropriate f/stop line (on the depth of field scale). By placing infinity at the far depth of field line we know it will also be in focus. Then the maximum depth of field will be utilized because it falls in front of infinity.

This means that the lens must be manually set to the determined distance (autofocus must be disengaged), and the exposure mode should be either "Aperture Priority" or "Manual." The photographer's control over lens settings is explained in the chapter on exposure modes; manual focus will be covered later in this chapter.

Once a photographer knows the theory he or she can be selective about depth of field. Vast distances or tiny slivers can be the planes of sharp focus. Focus to match a mood, focus to emphasize an object or focus to eliminate distractions. Another way to determine depth of field is with a book entitled *Kodak Pocket Photoguide,* which is available through Saunders (address on rear cover). This useful publication contains a depth of field dial that calculates depth of field for any focal length, at any lens opening.

Autofocus with the N6006

The Nikon N6006 is equipped with two autofocus modes, "single servo autofocus" and "continuous servo autofocus." In addition, the camera has a function that Nikon calls "focus tracking." If a subject is moving, focus tracking is automatically engaged. It analyzes the speed of the moving subject and anticipates the subject's position at the precise moment of exposure. Focus tracking works in both autofocus modes in conjunction with any film advance mode. Autofocus modes are selected with the Focus Mode Selector on the lower left front of the camera body.

In any mode, the camera's autofocus sensor focuses on the object that is seen by the rectangular area in the center of the viewfinder. The shutter cannot be released until the subject is in focus. This confirmation is indicated in the viewfinder. If only the

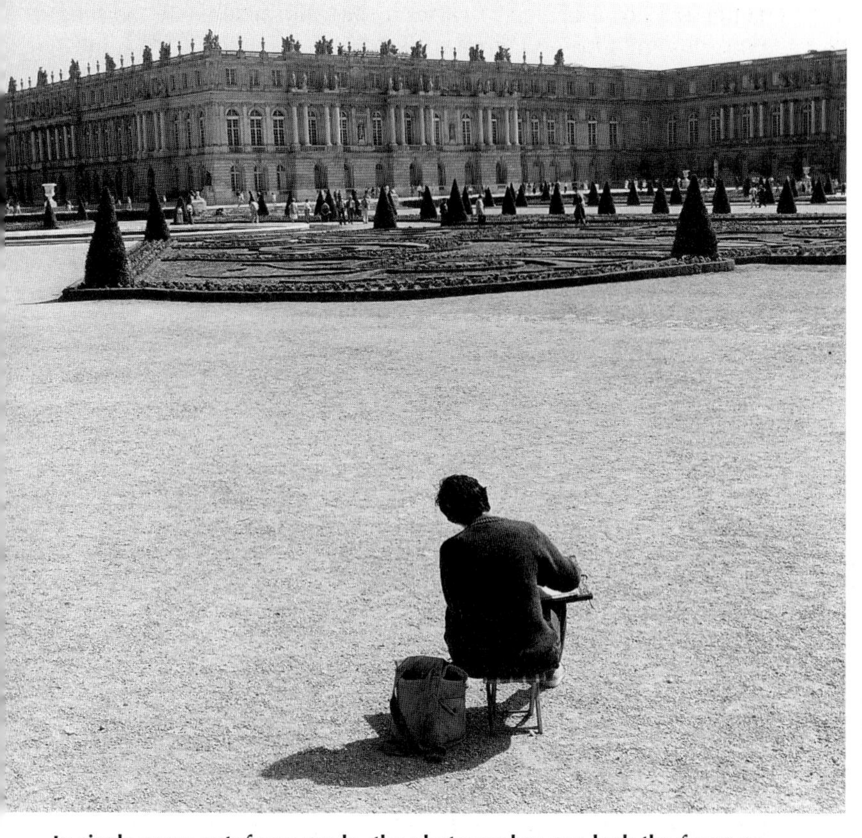

In single servo autofocus mode, the photographer can lock the focus on an off-center subject by keeping the shutter release button partially depressed. This allows the picture to be recomposed while the point of interest stays in sharp focus.

circle focus indicator is visible, that indicates that a stationary subject is in focus. If the same circle plus the two arrowheads can be seen, this means that focus tracking has been employed. (The circle and arrowheads will be used in manual focusing, but in a different way.)

Single Servo Autofocus: To engage this mode, set the Focus Mode Selector to "S". When the shutter release button is partially depressed, if the object is stationary, the autofocus locks and the focus-confirmation dot appears in the viewfinder. If the object moves before the shutter is tripped, remove your finger from the button, then lightly press it again to restart the process.

If the subject is moving when the button is depressed, focus tracking is automatically activated. Confirmation is verified when the focus dot plus the two arrowheads are visible in the viewfinder display. At that point the shutter may be tripped. If the subject stops moving before the shutter is tripped, the two arrowheads disappear and focus is locked. (The focus-confirmation dot remains.) When the focus locks in this way the shutter may still be released; but if the subject starts moving again, remove your finger then press again to restart the focus-tracking mechanism.

When the subject is not in the center of the viewfinder frame, this focusing mode works in the following manner: center the subject and depress the release button only far enough to activate the confirmation spot. Without removing the pressure from the shutter release button, recompose the image and shoot.

This procedure will lock focus, but not exposure. If you wish to lock both exposure and focus, see the section of this chapter called "Autofocus Lock." Nikon has a specific focusing program called autofocus lock, that locks both focus and exposure.

Continuous Servo Autofocus: For this mode, set the focus selector to "CF". When the camera is set in this mode and the subject is stationary, the confirmation circle will become visible. But if the camera-to-subject distance changes, while the shutter button is depressed, the focusing mechanism will constantly refocus to keep the subject in focus. In this mode, it is not possible to lock focus by partially depressing the shutter release.

The continuous servo autofocus mode was designed primarily for use with moving subjects. When the shutter release button is depressed lightly, and the tracking system senses movement, focus tracking becomes activated. Tracking will continue as long as the release button is partially depressed. The circle surrounded by the arrowheads gives confirmation. If the subject stops, the arrowheads disappear, but the dot remains. The exposure may be made at any time provided focus confirmation symbols are displayed.

Autofocus Lock (AF-L): AF-L should be used to lock both focus and exposure with an off-center subject To access this mode, press the shift button and the drive/AF-L button simultaneously. "AF-L" will be visible in the LCD panel and the viewfinder display. To cancel the AF-L mode, the same two buttons should be pressed again.

For stationary subjects, the camera is set in the single servo autofocus mode (S) and any automatic exposure mode. Center the subject in the focus brackets, lightly press the shutter release button lock focus and exposure, confirm focus, recompose and shoot.

Tips for Using Autofocus

Autofocus is a wonderful convenience, but it is not foolproof. The photographer needs to know the limitations of his equipment. Autofocus is no exception. Autofocus works best when it is focusing upon a subject that has strong contrast and vertical lines. Also, autofocus works well when operated in strong light. If those qualifications are not met, autofocus may not be able to cope. If the focus-confirmation dot blinks, the autofocus mechanism is having trouble performing its task. Many flash units such as the SB-25 have built-in focus-assist infrared illuminators. In low light situations, this will usually eliminate any problem focusing.

If the camera is being used in adequate light and the focus-confirmation dot flashes, be sure the focus brackets are covering an object with good vertical contrast. If there are strong horizontal lines to focus upon, turn the camera to the vertical position, lock the focus, recompose and shoot. An alternate autofocus procedure is to focus on another object, at the same distance as the subject, lock focus and shoot.

Sometimes it is better to disengage the autofocus system and focus manually. Situations where manual focus may be more effective include very dark subjects, low contrast subjects, a shiny subjects (with reflective surfaces), strongly backlit subjects or scenes on the other side of a window (bus windows, store windows, etc.).

Note: *Some filters may cause autofocus problems. Soft-focus filters, linear polarizers and other special effects filters are good examples of optical devices that may cause an autofocus malfunction. A linear polarizer should not be used on an autofocus camera; a circular polarizer will not interfere with the autofocus system.*

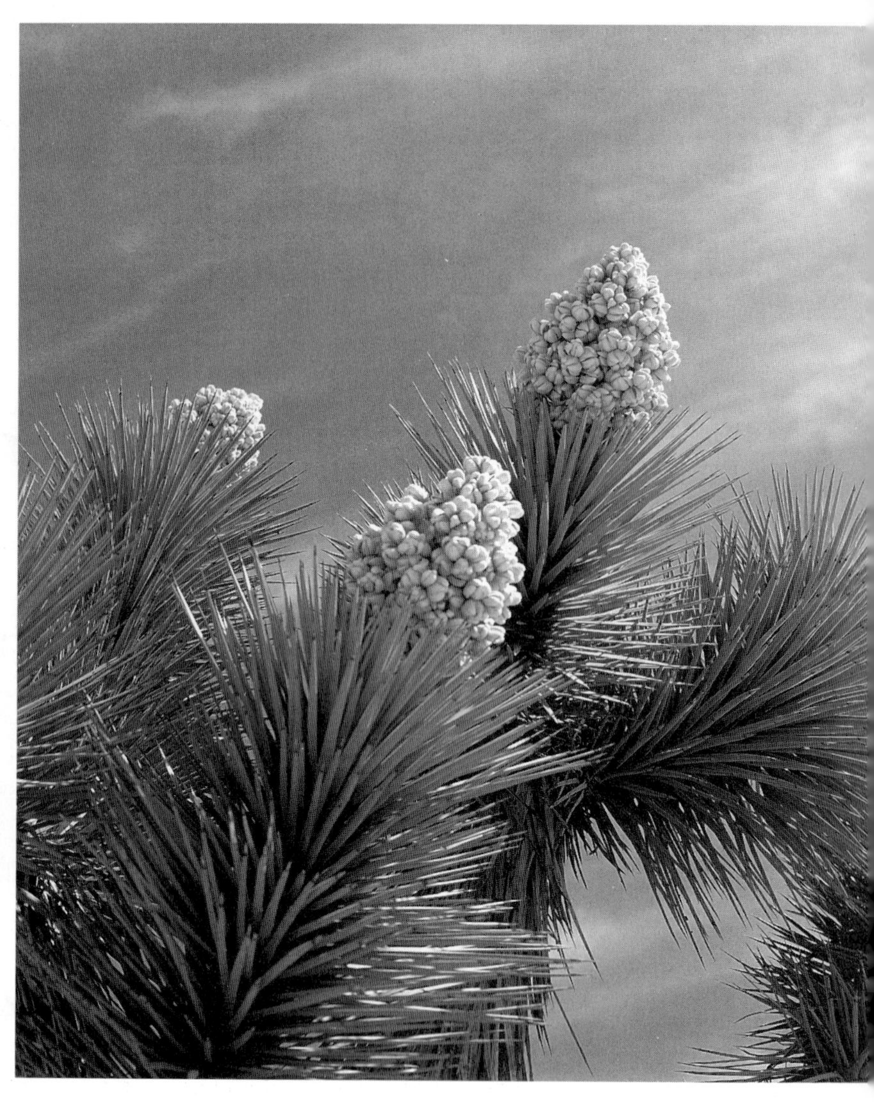

Subjects like this with clearly defined straight lines are excellent for practicing manual focusing.

Manual Focus with the N6006

The N6006 has two manual focusing aids: an electronic rangefinder plus visual confirmation via the viewfinder's matte fresnel field. To use manual focus, set the focus-mode selector to "M". If the lens in use has an "A-M" switch, set it to "M".

Manual Focus with the Electronic Rangefinder: Some lenses are not compatible with electronic rangefinder functions. Examples of these lenses include: PC (perspective-control) lenses, catadioptric (mirror) lenses and lenses with maximum apertures slower than f/5.6. Refer to the chart on page 145.

To use the rangefinder, check that the focus-mode selector and the lens "A-M" switch (if there is one) are on "M". Now look through the viewfinder and position the focus brackets on the subject. Lightly depress the shutter release button while rotating the lens focusing ring. The arrowhead in the viewfinder tells in which direction to turn the lens ring. If the other arrowhead appears, you have gone past the point of sharp focus. When sharp focus has been achieved, the arrowheads disappear and the focus-confirmation dot appears. When focus confirmation is achieved the exposure may be made.

Manual Focus Using the Matte Field: First, set the focus-mode selector to "M" and the lens "A-M" switch to "M" (if there is one). Second, look through the viewfinder and rotate the focusing ring until the subject appears clear and sharp in the viewfinder's matte focusing screen.

Focusing in this manner is easiest in strong light. Good eyesight is also a plus. Unfortunately, focusing with the matte section of the focusing screen is usually called for in unfavorable conditions. If this is new to you, practice first in strong light, then gradually test yourself in lower and lower light. Under some conditions you can test your results with the electronic rangefinder. If you are uncertain, and the image is important, try focus bracketing. This is accomplished in this manner: focus as best you can, and shoot; then turn the lens focusing ring slightly in one direction and shoot; then make another shot after turning the focusing ring slightly in the other direction.

Focusing the N6000

The N6000 comes with a focusing screen that Nikon calls a Type K screen. This is one of the most versatile focusing devices. It offers three distinct ways to focus: split-image focusing, microprism focusing and matte field focusing.

Split-Image Focusing: The center circle provides quick, precise, pinpoint focus on most subjects that reflect ample light to the viewfinder. This focusing circle is actually two half-circles. When the camera is held in a horizontal position the split is horizontal, so focusing is easiest if a vertical (or near vertical) line is the object focused upon. If the line focused upon is out of focus the top of the circle will not be aligned with the corresponding part seen in the lower half. To focus, turn the lens focusing ring until the image is aligned, top and bottom.

If no line in the subject is perpendicular to the finder line, turn the camera. If the shot is a vertical one, and all subject lines are vertical, turn the camera to the horizontal position.

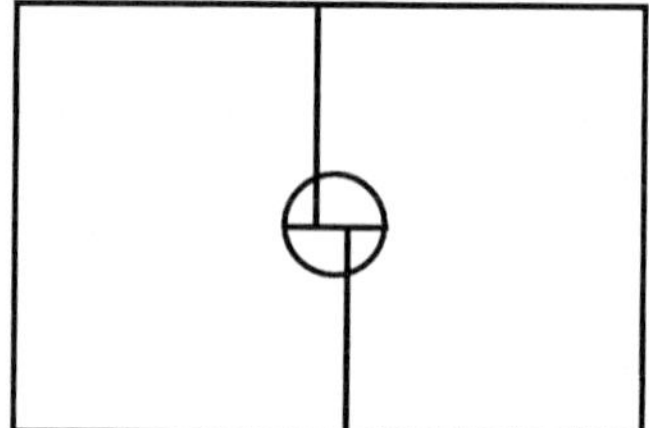

Out of Focus

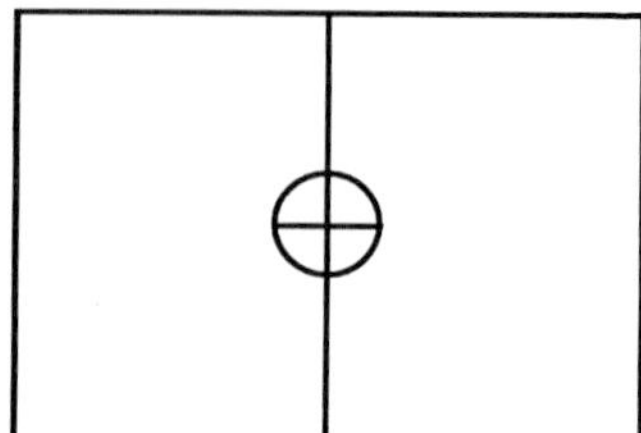

In Focus

When the split-image circle does not receive enough light, half of it will go dark. Slow lenses are usually the cause of this, but dense filters, extension tubes, bellows and other similar devices can also cause darkening. If darkening occurs, first try moving your eye. If the center of the eye is not centered in the viewfinder (both top-to-bottom and left-to-right) the darkening problem will be exaggerated. Move the camera in relation to the eye to see if the circle darkening will disappear. If the darkness moves from one half to the other, give up and try one of the alternate focusing methods.

Microprism Focusing: The doughnut-shaped area surrounding the split-image rangefinder is the microprism. It should be used with subjects that contain no distinct outlines or ones that have confusing edges. For example, a bunch of grapes.

Out of focus objects cause the microprism to shimmer or dance. Turn the lens focusing ring until the shimmering ceases. The subject is then in focus. Microprism focusing is very critical; do not expect the shimmering to entirely disappear from the object focused upon. It will only clear on one narrow plane. If, in a portrait, the subject's eye is in focus, the shimmering will be visible on the model's nose and ear. Practice with microprism focusing until you are comfortable with it. It is there to use in times when split-image focusing will not work.

Matte-Field Focusing: The matte field in the N6006 and the N6000 are identical. Matte field focusing is especially helpful when long telephoto lenses, telescopes and microscopes are used.

Tips on Manual Focusing

The same optical rules apply to autofocus and manual focus systems. Most scenes present little difficulty, where focusing is concerned, but sometimes just the right trick will come in handy.

A zoom lens will yield its most critical focus if set at the lens' longest focal length. Position it there for the easiest and most accurate focus then zoom down to the desired focal length for composition. Before using this technique, be sure the lens will retain focus throughout its entire zoom range. Some low-cost, aftermarket lenses will not. This is easy to test by focusing on a large, well-lighted object, then while zooming down observe any shift of focus (using the clear-matte field).

When photographing a dark subject, especially in low light, locate a bright object at the same distance as the subject and focus on it. If that fails, a flashlight may be the answer. Place it at the subject, with its bulb pointing in the direction of the camera. Focus on the flashlight's bulb, remove it and shoot. A small flashlight carried in your camera bag will come in handy countless times for both photographic and non-photographic uses. And of course, if all else fails, guess the distance and set it on the lens' focusing scale manually, then bracket the focus. Sometimes,

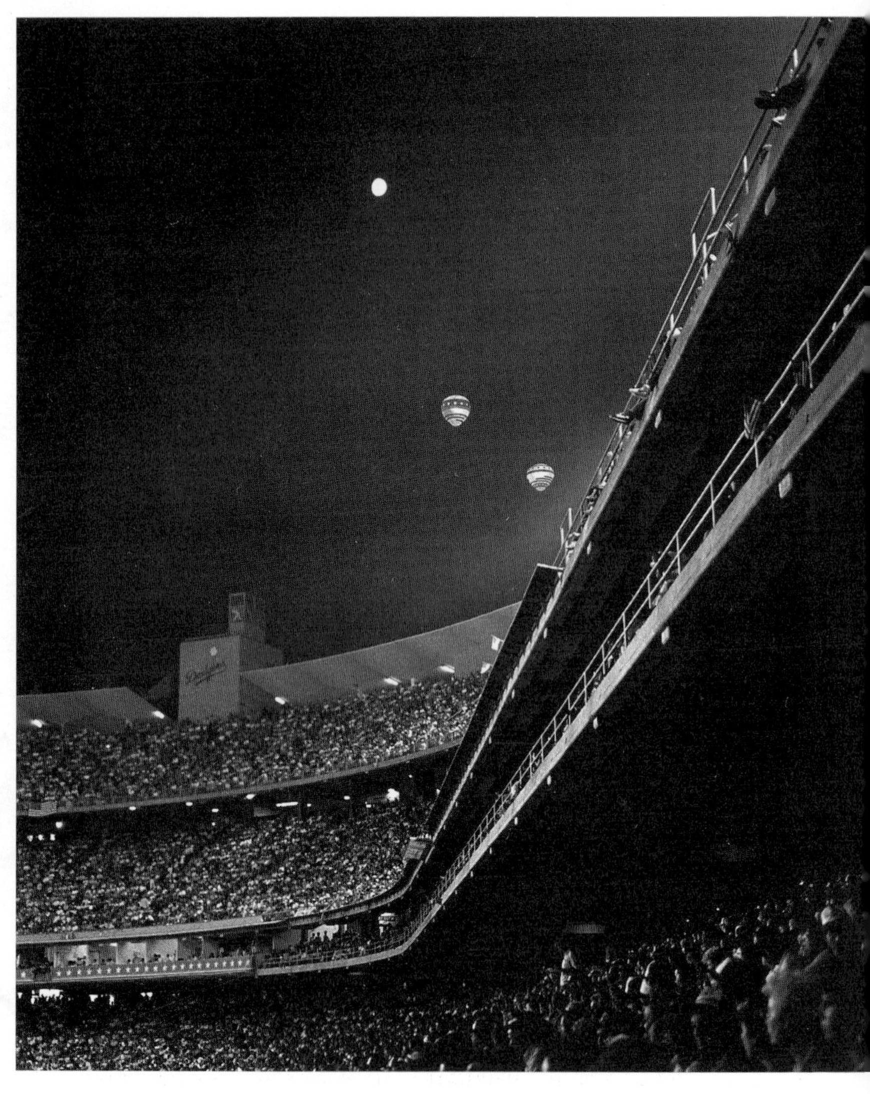

A monopod was used for this photograph taken at Dodger Stadium. A tripod was not allowed in the arena, but camera support was essential for this long exposure.

when photographing a moving object, it is better to pre-focus on a given spot and shoot when the subject reaches that point. For example, focus on the finish line, not the contestants.

Using the Self-Timer

The N6000-series cameras have the ability to take a single self-timer shot or two consecutive self-timer exposures in one single operation. Before taking the picture, place the camera on a steady support; the best choice would be a good tripod. Compose and focus on your subject, leaving room for yourself, if you plan to jump into the picture. Lightly depress the shutter release button to confirm satisfactory exposure.

One-shot self-timer operation: Depress the self-timer button and rotate the command dial until the desired delay time is displayed on the LCD panel. Times between two and thirty seconds, can be selected. The LCD display is the only location of self-timer information. It will display the symbol "1F" (single frame), the self-timer symbol and the length of the delay in seconds.

To take the picture, fully depress the shutter release button while holding the self-timer button down. At this time, the self-timer begins to blink and the timer counts down. The people being photographed can see the red LED on the face of the camera light up; it is located just below the shutter release button. This LED is also blinking, and the pulses will quicken in the final two seconds prior to the actual exposure.

Two-shot self-timer operation: Press the self-timer button while rotating the command dial in a counterclockwise direction past the 30 second setting. "2F" will appear in the LCD panel. The first shot will occur approximately ten seconds after the shutter is tripped and the second shot will be approximately five seconds later.

To cancel the self-timer operation: The self-timer can be cancelled even after it has begun to countdown; just press the self-timer button. To confirm that the operation is cancelled, observe the LED display.

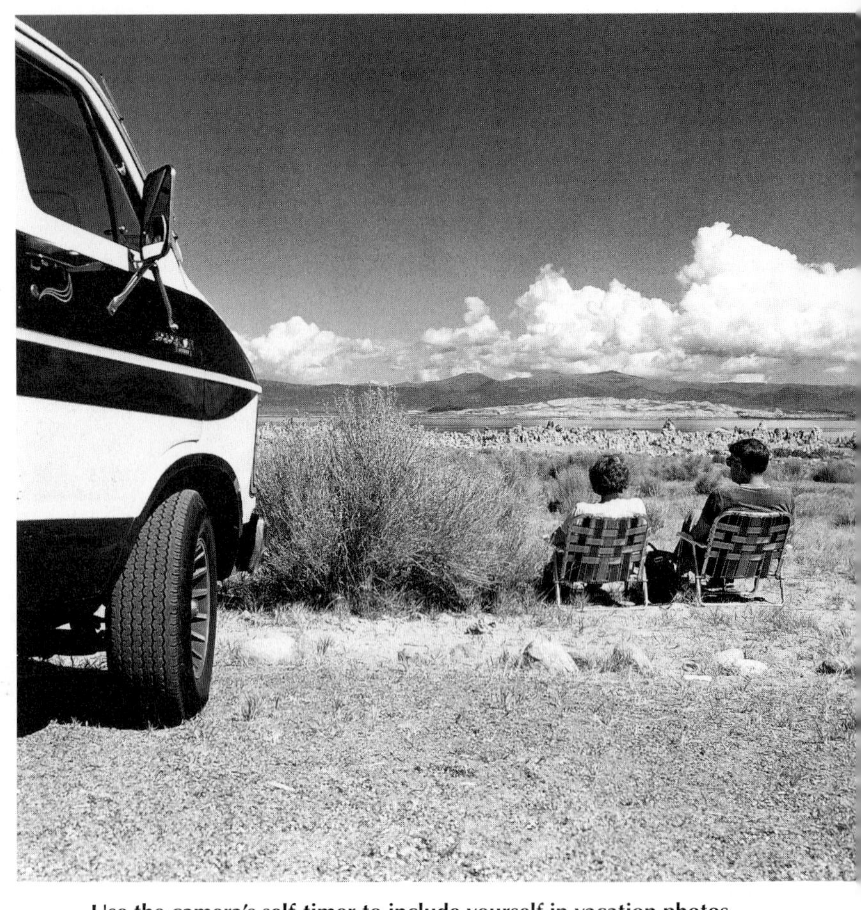

Use the camera's self-timer to include yourself in vacation photos.

Note: *Any time the viewfinder is not shielded from the light, as it usually is by the photographer's head, the eyepiece cover, DK-5 should be used. This device keeps light from entering the camera via the eyepiece. Light entering the system via this route may cause erroneous exposure settings. Consequently, always cover the eyepiece when using the self-timer. If the DK-5 cover is not at hand, any substitute may be used.*

The "Bulb" Setting

The slowest shutter speed on N6000-series cameras is one second. When longer exposures are required, the bulb setting allows the photographer to hold the shutter open for as long as necessary. Long exposures are often used because they produce unique and unusual images. They make the viewer of the photograph see the scene in a way that is totally foreign. The human eye, when viewing the original scene, usually cannot register the effects that long exposures produce. An interesting subject for time exposures is moving cars at night. Time exposures take some practice and experience, but the images created can be rewarding. Try some!

Setting the camera: Manual exposure mode must be used with the bulb setting. Set the exposure mode to "M", and then rotate the command dial until "bulb" appears in the displays. Set the lens to any aperture that is required for the desired depth of field; just remember, the smaller the aperture the longer the exposure time. Once the subject is composed and focused on, the photographer simply needs to press the shutter release and hold it for the entire duration of the exposure.

The camera's metering system will not work with the bulb setting. An alternate method of exposure metering must be used. That can be as scientific as using a separate, handheld light meter or as simple as making a guess. It is highly recommended that when guessing, several different exposure times be tried.

The most useful accessories for time exposures are a good tripod and a cable release. The Nikon N6000 series cameras are some of the few modern cameras that use a common mechanical cable release (Nikon Accessory AR-3). Most require unique electronic models that are not inexpensive. See also, page 110 and 157.

Note: *Time exposures subject the battery to constant drain for the entire duration of the exposure. Nikon claims that the N6006 can be used for seven hours (in the time exposure mode) with a fresh battery, while the N6000 will perform for up to ten hours, under the same conditions.*

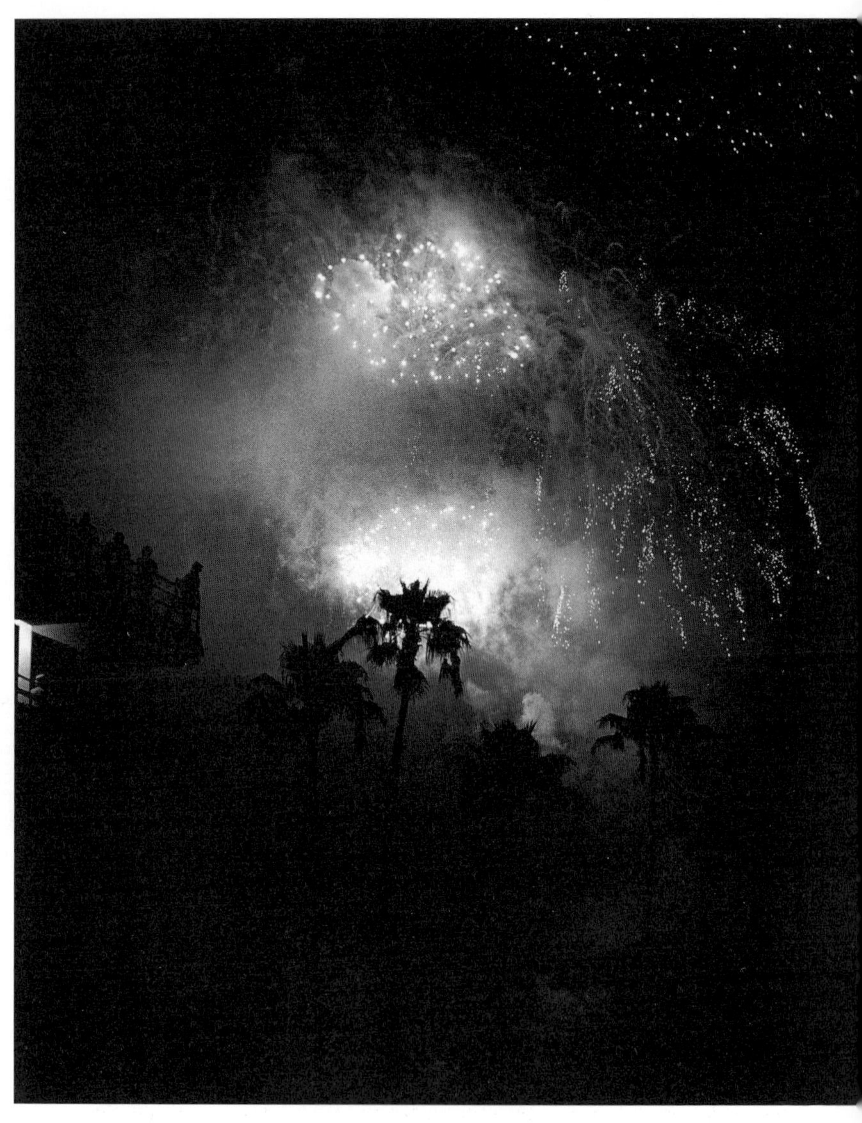

A tripod, a cable release, an aperture of f/5.6 and the "bulb" setting are a good place to start for taking photos of fireworks such as this.

Automatic Bracketing

This mode is used when different exposures of the same subject are desired. Either three or five exposures can be made. One frame is taken based on the camera's meter reading and either two or four additional frames are under- and overexposed using set exposure compensation increments. We will see how these settings are accomplished soon.

Automatic Bracketing works with any of the automatic exposure modes ("P", "Pm", "S" and "A"). In the "P" and "Pm" mode, both shutter speed and aperture will be changed when bracketing is used. Aperture will be changed when the camera is in the "S" mode and the bracketing sequence commences. It therefore follows that the shutter speed will vary when bracketing is called for and the camera is in the "A" mode. If the camera is in the manual mode, and auto exposure bracketing is engaged, exposure compensation will not occur.

Auto bracketing is a substitute for problem-solving. If you are thinking of using it, you are already aware of a possible exposure problem. A little additional thinking should guide you in the proper direction. Will normal meter settings lead to underexposure, proper exposure or overexposure? By now you know the answer; you do not have to guess, do you? Everyone needs to make insurance exposures, but why not make them in the correct direction? If underexposure is possible, is it not better to make one normal exposure and four on the plus side, instead of one normal, two under and two over?

Setting the Auto Bracketing Function

To engage the auto exposure bracketing function, follow this procedure. While pressing the shift button, depress the "BKT" button. The viewfinder display now shows a blinking +/-, and "BKT" and +/- flash in the LCD display. "BKT" stops flashing when the meter is turned off, but remains visible on the display.

Now, while depressing the "BKT" button, turn the command dial to set the number of exposures you wish to make (up to five). Next, with your finger removed from the "BKT" button, rotate the command dial to set the degree of compensation required. The film counter portion on the LCD panel shows the number of exposures in the series (instead of the number of frames taken on

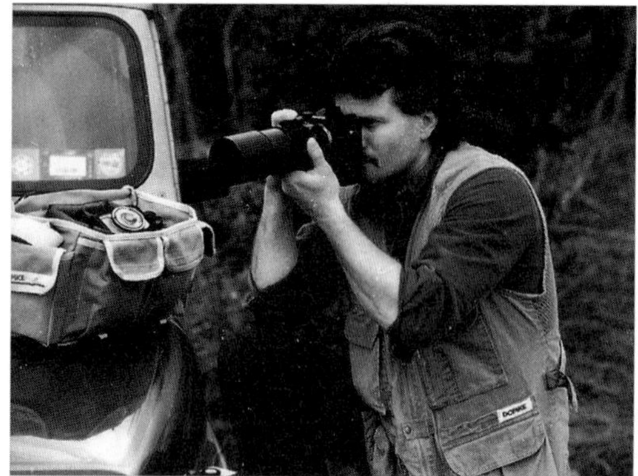

An example of an exposure series using the auto bracket feature with a normal exposure (middle), 1/2 stop underexposure (top) and 1/2 stop overexposure (bottom).

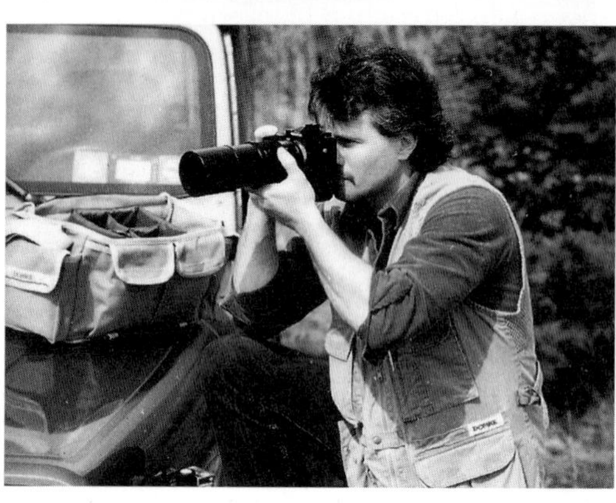

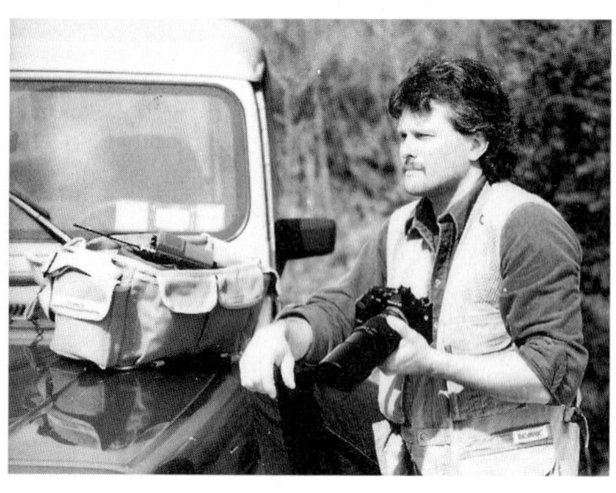

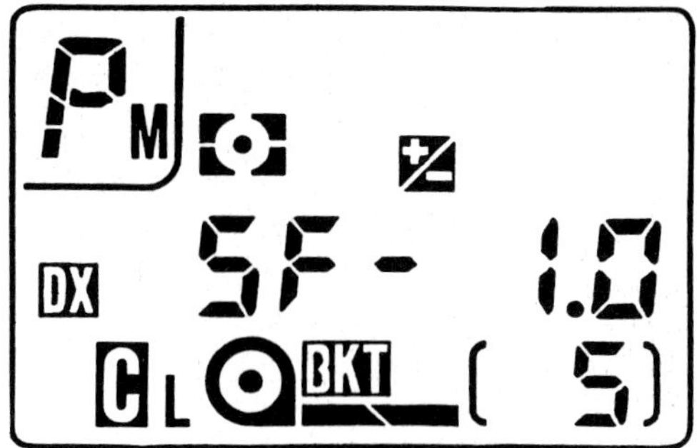

In auto bracket mode, the LCD panel shows the number of exposures in the series and the amount of exposure compensation selected. The readout 5F - 1.0 pictured here shows a five exposure series with each exposure differing by one stop.

the roll). And BKT plus +/- are also displayed, as well as the amount of compensation selected.

When the shutter is released, the bracketing series begins. The LCD counter will count down the number of exposures remaining, until the entire sequence is completed. The exposure sequence works in this manner: first the underexposure(s), then the normal exposure then the overexposure(s).

If the film advance is set to "S", the shutter release button must be pressed for each exposure. If it is set to either "CL" or "CH", the entire series can be exposed without removing your finger from the shutter release. If your finger is removed from the shutter release before the entire series is completed, the sequence will stop. Tripping the shutter release again will complete the series. When the series is completed, all the bracketing symbols will disappear and the camera will automatically revert to the original settings prior to bracketing.

To cancel the automatic bracketing: Before or during the operation, press the shift button and the BKT button simultaneously. What if the film reaches the end of the roll before the bracketing sequence is completed? After reloading, the sequence can continue with no additional settings necessary.

Auto Bracketing with Flash

Auto exposure bracketing will also work with flash photography, if the flash is Nikon-dedicated. Bracketing adjusts the amount of flash output in any of the camera's modes including "M". If any exposure compensation is set, on either camera or flash, and automatic exposure bracketing is also employed, the compensations are additive.

Using Exposure Compensation

This procedure will allow the user to set exposure compensation in one-third stop increments up to plus or minus five stops. Exposure compensation is an acquired skill; it starts out being a guessing game and becomes refined with experience. But it can never be a precise science, and even the proficient get fooled occasionally. Therefore, it is advisable to hedge your bets by bracketing your exposures.

When experience takes a photographer beyond totally automatic exposure, this is a good, safe and relatively simple deviation. Anyone who read the section "How Meters Work" in the previous chapter should usually be able to determine when automatic exposure is likely to fail and whether plus or minus compensation is needed. But how much adjustment is needed? Again, experience is the only guide. Most people use the trial and error system, learning as they go.

To activate exposure compensation: To engage exposure compensation, while pressing the exposure compensation button (marked +/-), rotate the command dial until the desired correction has been set. The displays will now say "+/-", the analog scale (EV-1 to EV+1) will be visible and the compensation value (from -5 to +5) will also be displayed. As stated earlier, the compensation is adjustable in one-third f/stop increments.

While the camera is set for exposure compensation, the "+/-" blinks. This blinking is a welcome reminder because, once the camera has been set for exposure compensation, it will remain fixed until exposure compensation has been canceled.

To disengage the compensation function: Press the "+/-" button then set the compensation to zero. The "+/-" will disappear from the displays to indicate the camera's meter has been zeroed.

Hasn't everyone on a cruise ship attempted to photograph a similar scene? This shot was successful in spite of its extreme backlighting because the photographer used his knowledge of photography in applying the N6006's exposure compensation feature. ⇨

Motor Drive Modes

The N6000-series cameras have an excellent built-in motordrive to advance the film automatically. Depressing the "DRIVE" button and turning the command input control dial selects one of three film advance speeds. The three advance modes available are "S", "CL" and "CH". These letters appear in the lower left corner of the LCD panel. In the "S" mode, is fired a single exposure each time the shutter release button is depressed. The "CL" mode will fire a maximum of 1.2 fps (frames per second) and the "CH" 2.0 fps for as long as the shutter release button is held down. These firing rates do not take into account the need to refocus if the subject is moving.

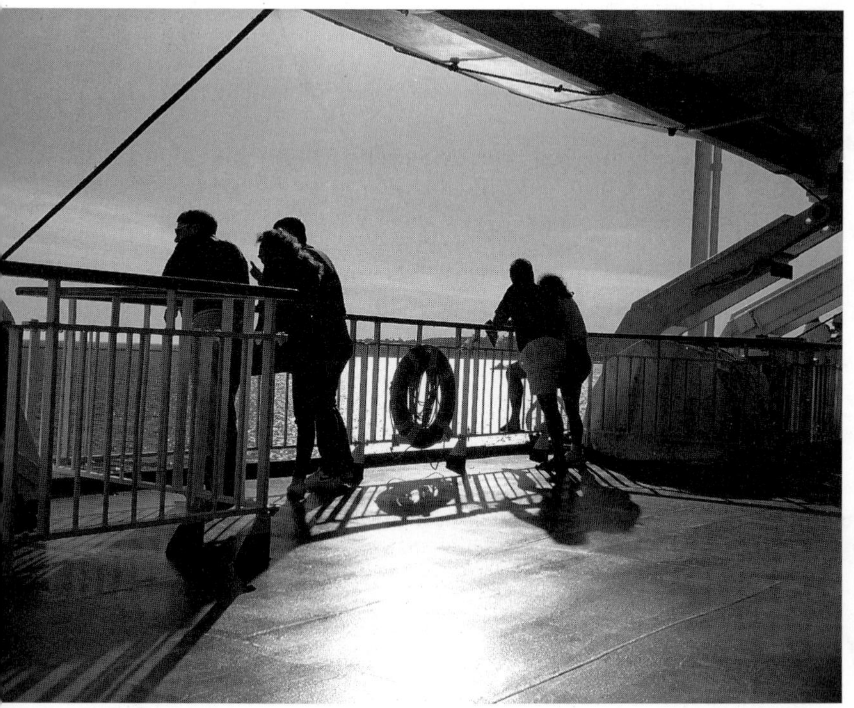

N8008s Camera Controls

The introduction of the N8008 and N8008s brought genuine excitement to the Nikon line. Heralded as "high performance autofocus SLRs", it is already hard to remember that these cameras came from an era when manual cameras ruled supreme among professionals. TTL flash metering, a built-in motordrive and the real biggie - autofocus, all encased in a polycarbonate housing, were viewed with skepticism by traditional photographers of the day. At first, the N8008s was received with apprehension, but in just a short period of time it was replacing the F3 in many camera bags. Photographers quickly realized the benefits of the N8008s' sophisticated technology.

What's in the N8008s for such a claim to be made? Through-the-lens flash technology with a top flash sync of 1/250, matrix metering with a top shutter speed of 1/8000, a high-eyepoint finder and a high speed built-in motordrive are all combined in a compact body. It is these features, the technology that makes them work and their easy application by the photographer that has created such a large and loyal following for the N8008s.

As with any tool, whether photographic or not, complete understanding is essential to achieve maximum effectiveness and results. Where instruction books might shed some light on the mechanics, they often leave out the insight on how and why to apply a particular feature. In addition to explaining the ins and outs of the N8008s, this book also describes how and why to apply the features so the photographer can make the most of this incredible camera system.

Note: *All discussions include both the N8008 and N8008s. However, the N8008s is the more advanced of the two models and has several upgrades. Where there is a deviation in systems, special mention will be made.*

N8008s LCD Panel

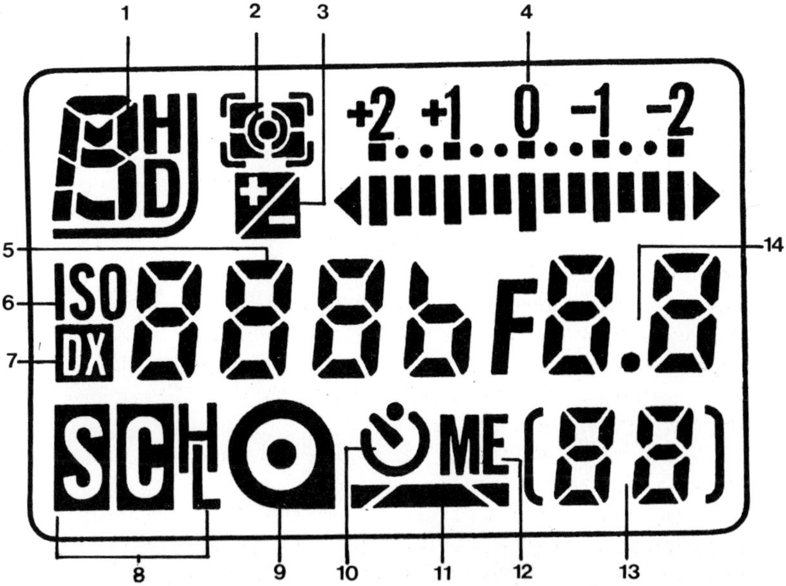

1. Camera exposure mode
2. Metering mode
3. Exposure compensation indicator
4. Analog exposure display
5. Shutter speed/ISO film speed
6. ISO setting method
7. DX-coded film speed setting
8. Film advance mode
9. Film loading
10. Self-timer
11. Film advance and rewind
12. Multiple exposure
13. Frame counter/frames for multiple exposure/self-timer countdown
14. Aperture/exposure compensation

The On/Off Switch

The on/off switch is pretty self-explanatory. But the beeper function connected to it needs a little explaining. By sliding the switch to the beeper symbol, the camera will talk to you with a beep. The beep can signal the following operations: the end of a roll of film, completed film rewind, and self-timer countdown.

The beep sounds to warn of the following problems, a shutter speed is being used slower than 1/30 (in automatic exposure modes), when the attached flash is in "rear" curtain mode, if "HI"

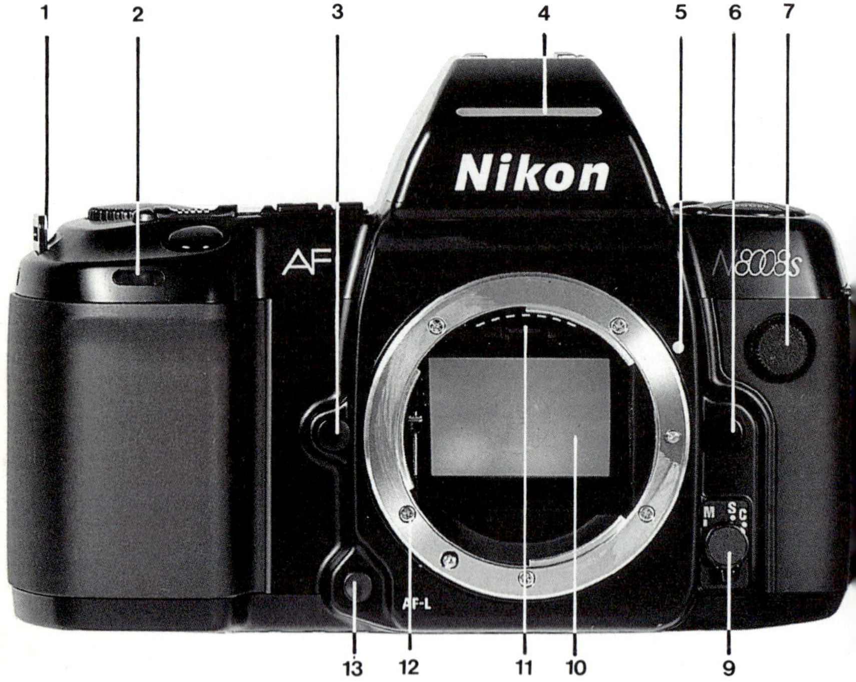

1 2 3 4 5 6 7

Nikon
AF
N8008s
M S C
AF-L

13 12 11 10 9

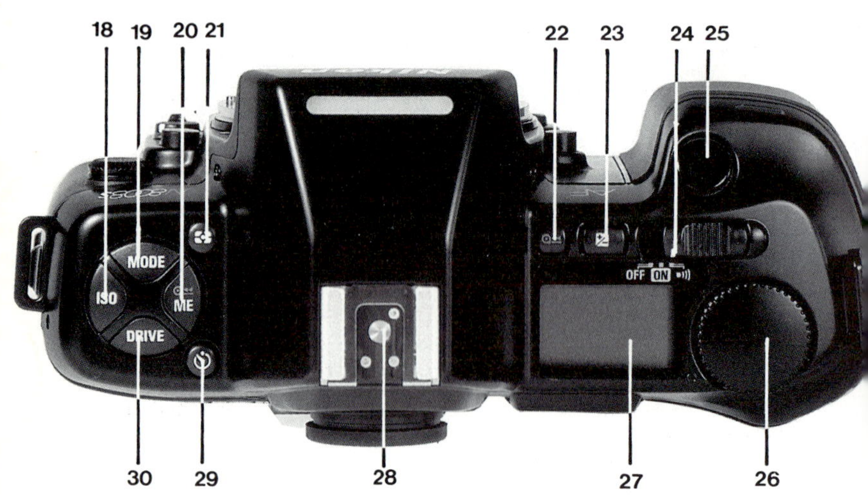

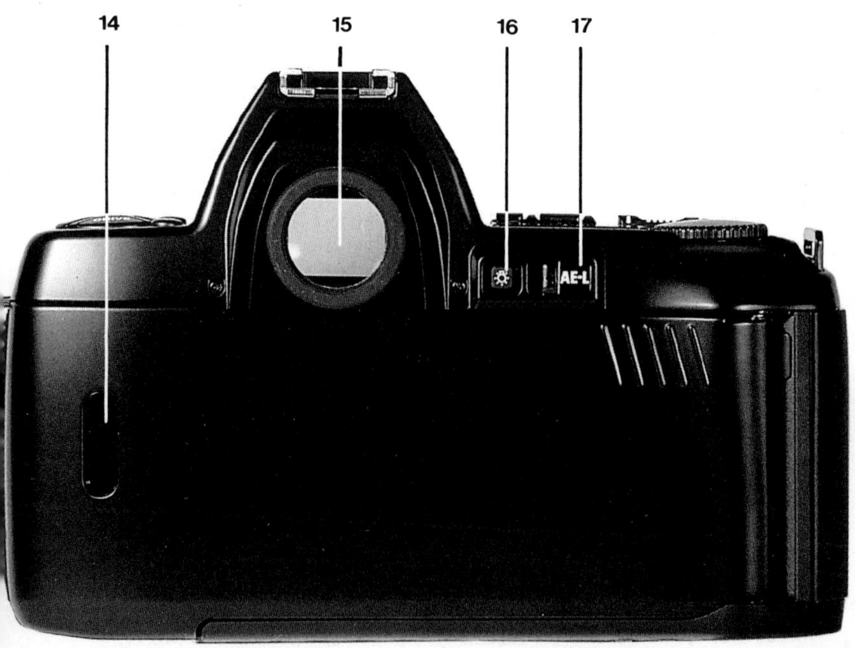

1. Camera strap eyelet
2. Self-timer light
3. Depth of field preview button
4. LCD illumination window
5. Lens mounting index
6. Lens release button
7. Remote control terminal (covered)
8. Camera back release
9. Focus mode selector
10. Reflex mirror
11. Autofocus coupling
12. CPU contacts
13. Autofocus lock button
14. Film cassette window
15. Viewfinder
16. Viewfinder illumination button
17. Auto exposure lock lever
18. Film speed button
19. Exposure mode button
20. Multiple exposure/film rewind button
21. Metering system button
22. Film rewind button
23. Exposure compensation button
24. Power switch
25. Shutter release button
26. Command input control dial
27. LCD panel
28. Hot shoe
29. Self-timer button
30. Film advance mode button

or "Lo" appear in any exposure mode, if the lens is not closed down to its minimum aperture when in use with one of the program modes, if the camera is set to DX mode but the film does not have a DX code or when film is misloaded.

LCD Display

The LCD panel on the top right of the camera is where everything is displayed. This includes the metering mode, exposure mode, film speed setting, film advance mode, self-timer, exposure compensation, shutter speed, aperture setting, exposure compensation, frame counter, multiple exposure, film rewind and film installation.

Film Loading

To open the camera back, pinch the two sliding levers on the left side of the camera together. Place the film cassette into the film cassette chamber on the left side of the camera and pull the leader over to the right to the red square. Be careful not to touch the shutter curtain or film pressure plate in the process. Close the camera back and press the shutter release, the camera will automatically advance the film to frame one.

The film installation symbol, a film cassette with the leader sticking out, indicates that film has been correctly loaded. If the film is not loaded correctly, the symbol will blink when the shutter release button is depressed. And if no film is loaded in the camera, an "E" will appear in the frame counter.

The ISO Setting

The "ISO" button sets the speed of the film into the camera's computer. It can be done two ways, setting the ISO manually or allowing the camera to set it with "DX". The N8008s has a range of ISO 6 to 6400. You can manually set the film speed to any standard ISO number within that range. This is preferred by some photographers who do not want to use the manufacturer's rating to expose their film. For example, underexposing slide film slightly for more saturated colors.

In the "DX" mode, the camera will read the DX coding on the side of the film cassette and automatically set the ISO for you. An "Err" message will appear if the film is not DX coded or is outside the DX code range. In this mode, any compensation for exposure would be dialed in via the exposure compensation dial or through the shutter speed/aperture combo. The DX mode is for those who constantly change film types and don't want to think about changing the film speed.

Film Advance

The N8008s has an excellent built-in motordrive that automatically advances the film. Depressing the "DRIVE" button and turning the command input control dial selects one of three film advance speeds. The three advance modes available are "S", "CL" and "CH". These letters appear in the lower left corner of the LCD panel and are selected as mentioned previously. In the "S" mode, the camera fires each time the shutter release button is depressed completely. The firing rate or frames per second (fps) depends entirely on the speed of your finger. The "CL" mode will fire a maximum of 2.0 fps and the "CH" 3.3 fps for as long as the shutter release button is held down. These firing rates require shutter speeds greater than 1/125 and do not take into account having to autofocus if that mode is activated. These variables can slow down the actual firing rate.

The camera can be set to either "CL" or "CH" and still fire only one frame at a time. Remember, to fire continually you must hold down the shutter release button. If after the first frame the shutter release is not depressed, it will not fire. This allows you to shoot single frames and still take advantage of the motor drive when needed.

Film Rewind

On the "ME" button is a red film canister symbol with two arrows. This same symbol can be found just to the right of the prism above the LCD panel. When these two buttons are depressed, the camera automatically rewinds the film. With fresh batteries, this takes approximately 17 seconds to accomplish. During the process, the frame counter in the LCD panel will count down the number of frames left to be rewound.

The film leader is pulled completely into the cassette upon rewinding. Some photographers prefer the leader be left out of the cassette after rewinding. This can be accomplished by either popping open the film back at the appropriate time (watch the frame counter) or by having Nikon modify the camera to leave the leader sticking out after rewinding.

Multiple Exposure

The "ME" button serves another function - the one for which it is named. When the "ME" Button is pressed, the multiple exposure function is called up. The film is not moved during this operation, only the shutter is cocked and fired, so multiple images can be overlapped on a single frame of film.

Turning the command input control dial sets the number of multiple exposures up to nine. The letters "ME" along with the number of frames selected appears in the lower right corner of the LCD panel, but not in the viewfinder.

The actual number of exposures taken can be increased beyond what is set on the camera. The multiple exposure counter on the LCD panel counts down the number of exposures before returning to normal operation. If watched carefully, when the multiple frame counter displays a 1, the "ME" button can depressed and the command input control dial turned, changing the frame count. This can be done as often as desired in any exposure or metering mode, but exposure calculation is up to the photographer. The camera cannot figure it out for you. Exposure is cumulative as multiple images are "layered" on a single frame of film. Underexposing each consecutive image slightly may produce better results.

If during a multiple exposure run you decide or need to go back to regular shooting, depressing the "ME" button and turning the command input control dial in the opposite direction will cancel any multiple exposures left.

Resetting the Camera

Pressing the "MODE and "DRIVE" buttons simultaneously activates the camera's default settings - Dual Program (PD), single frame film advance (S) and matrix metering. Any other feature or function dialed into the camera such as continuous film advance, exposure compensation, or multiple exposure will be canceled.

Metering Modes

Depressing the matrix symbol on the left and then turning the command input control dial is required to access, matrix, center-weighted and spot metering. On the LCD panel next to the exposure mode is the metering mode display. It will change from a matrix symbol (matrix metering), a dot between two brackets (center-weighted mode) and a dot (spot metering). This information is not displayed in the viewfinder.

Self-timer

Depressing the timer symbol accesses the self-timer. Turning the command input control dial allows you to set the self-timer for 2 to 30 seconds. Turning the dial one notch more access a two frame feature. In this mode, the camera will take two frames via the self-timer. The first frame is taken approximately ten seconds after the shutter is depressed and the second five seconds after the first.

To start the self-timer, depress the timer symbol and lightly press the shutter release. When activated, a red light in the handle of the camera flashes to indicate the self timer has been turned on. Remember that if in any exposure mode other than manual, use the eyepiece shield (DK-8) to prevent extraneous light from entering the prism. The self-timer also works with a flash attached.

A practical use for the self-timer is those instances when a cable release is needed but not available. To avoid touching the camera prior to exposure, set the self-timer to 20 seconds, depress the buttons to activate and let it do the rest. A period of 20 seconds is plenty of time for the camera to become still after you take your hands away.

Power Consumption

The N8008s runs on four AA batteries. The number of rolls you can expect to shoot from a fresh set of batteries depends on the mode of operation. By focusing the lens manually, approximately 160 rolls can be fired from a single set of batteries. Using the autofocus all the time can cut that number down to 105. What shortens the life of a set of batteries below these numbers is how much "play" time your batteries receive. Folks tend to play with the autofocus, focusing on different subjects or experimenting. Battery life is rarely as great as these numbers, so don't be upset if your performance is only half of what is stated here.

Battery Status

One other function of the LCD panel is to indicate battery power. Lightly depressing the shutter release activates the camera, causing the LCD to come on immediately. The display should remain on for 8 seconds once your finger is off the shutter release button. If it turns off immediately, the batteries need changing. If the LCD display should blink while you finger is on the shutter release, it indicates insufficient battery power is available. And if nothing comes on, the batteries are dead.

There is another possibility if the camera does not come on or displays unusual readings. The camera may have been shorted out. The three computers in the N8008s are not grounded which leaves them vulnerable to static electricity. To correct this, remove the batteries from the camera body for thirty seconds and then put them back. If that doesn't clear the problem, the batteries (or the camera) are truly dead.

Viewfinder Displays

The bottom line of the viewfinder displays a limited amount of information. The indicators for the focusing system are on to the left, the exposure mode is to the right of them, then the shutter speed and aperture (if lens with a CPU is in use), and then the analog metering scale depending on the exposure mode in use.

To the far right, the "+/-" symbol is displayed if exposure compensation is in use. If a flash is attached, a red lightning bolt on the extreme right will light when the flash is ready and indicate either correct or incorrect exposure when the flash is fired.

This viewfinder display will automatically illuminate in low light situations to aid in reading the display. You can also turn on the viewfinder light manually. Next to the AE-L button on the back of the camera is a button with a starburst. Pressing this activates the viewfinder light. The light remains on in either instance for as long as the shutter release is depressed and for eight seconds afterwards.

Viewfinder Image

The image through the viewfinder of the N8008s is only 92% of what is actually captured by the film. What this means is there

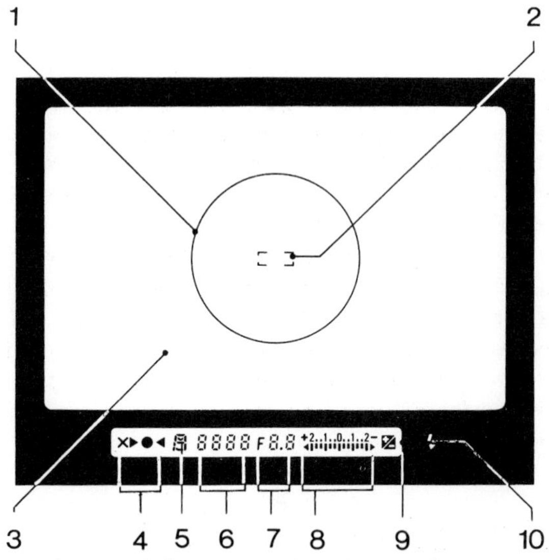

1. **12 mm reference circle**
2. **Focus brackets**
3. **Matte fresnel field**
4. **Focus arrow indicators**
5. **Exposure mode**
6. **Shutter speed/ ISO film speed**
7. **Aperture/exposure compensation**
8. **Analog exposure display**
9. **Exposure compensation indicator**
10. **Flash ready light**

will actually be more in the photograph than you saw through the camera. This can play tricks with you in two ways. One, extraneous items can be captured in the photograph not seen through the viewfinder. Two, things will seem bigger in the viewfinder then they turn out to be on film. Experience will teach you how to see what will actually be in the photograph.

Depth of Field Preview

The N8008s has a feature that is quite helpful, but often overlooked, depth of field preview. Depth of field preview permits the photographer to view the scene with everything that will be in focus for the selected aperture. Located next to the lens barrel on the front of the camera is the depth of field preview button. Pushing this button depresses the automatic diaphragm lever in the lens and closes down the aperture. This causes the viewfinder to go dark and makes it difficult to judge the image. Using this technique to see depth of field requires practice if the photographer is to make effective use of it. It only works in aperture priority or manual exposure modes. When depressed, the aperture setting on the LCD panel and in the viewfinder reads "F--".

One Final Note on the N8008s: The only other difference between the N8008 and N8008s occurs when the MF-21 back is attached. When using the auto bracketing feature with the MF-21 attached, the N8008s will fire off all the frames for the auto bracket sequence by simply depressing the shutter release. (Film advance mode must be CL or CH.) The N8008 requires that the shutter release be depressed for each exposure.

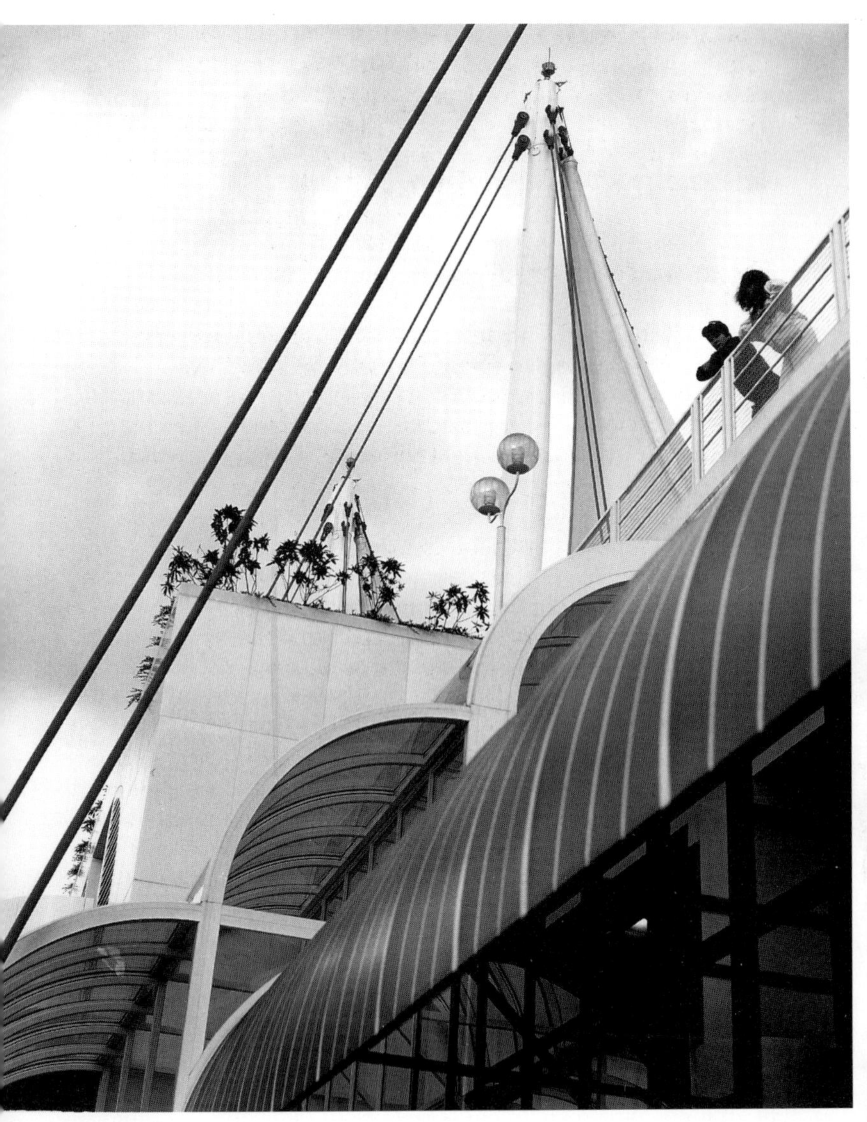

Photographs of interesting architectural structures are often improved by including people in the composition.

Advanced Functions

The Autofocus Revolution

Up until the release of the N8008, Nikon's autofocus offering had been dismal. The early autofocus cameras, the F3AF and N2020, worked well but were technologically weak and by no means lit the imagination of photographers. The N8008 and N8008s did, and still do to this day! There are many attributes which contribute to the success of its autofocus system. Some information about its operating system is strictly for techno-wizards, but there are practical features needed by all in everyday shooting.

Autofocus Mechanics

The heart of the N8008s autofocus system is the Advanced AM200 Autofocus Module. The AM200 module is a one piece optical block packed with state-of-the-art, newly designed (as of 1988), Charge-Coupled Device (CCD) sensors. The two hundred CCDs in the AM200 (standing for Autofocus Module with 200 CCDs) represented the largest number in an SLR at the time, giving the N8008s the edge over other autofocus cameras. In essence, the N8008s has superior response speed and enhanced focus detection capability, especially in extremely low light.

The way this all works is really amazing. Keep in mind this all happens at the speed of light. Light passes through the lens, then passes through a 6 x 10mm sub-mirror. The surface of the main mirror reflects 65% of the light striking it upwards to the matrix meter sensor and viewfinder image located in the prism. The remaining 35% passes through the 6 x 10mm hole for autofocus detection.

The sub-mirror is attached to the back of the main reflex mirror at an approximate angle of 80 degrees (it folds up out of the way behind the main mirror when the mirror raises to take a photograph. The light passing through the lens and main mirror bounces off the sub-mirror to strike the focal point of the AM200

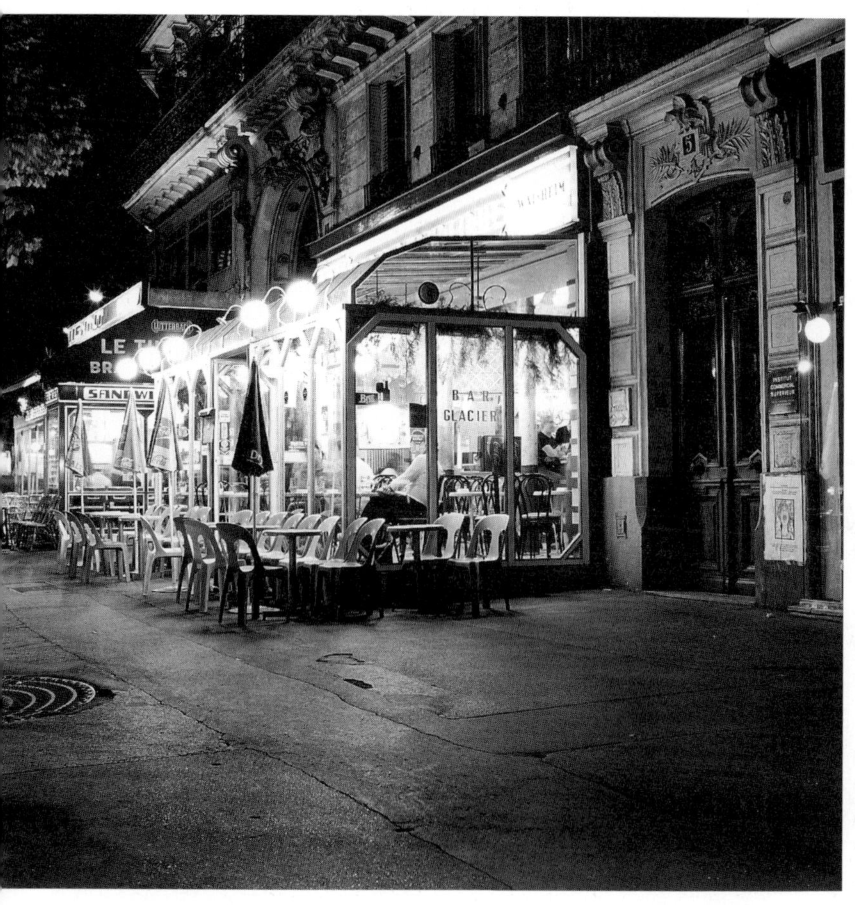

Even brightly light night scenes such as this Paris bistro are no problem for Nikon's sophisticated autofocus system.

module. This point is the geometric equivalent of the plane of focus where the lens focuses the image on the film. At this point, the light diverges into two paths. The light then passes through a special filter which filters out and eliminates ultraviolet (UV) light. This filter can be seen at the base of the mirror box near the shutter curtain when the camera is set on "bulb", holding the mirror up and out of the way. The high frequency of ultraviolet light, if allowed to pass, would confuse the sensor which is looking for lower frequency, infrared light.

The light path then travels through an optical block. The block's top spherical surface acts as a field condenser lens, enhancing the image stability. The single optical block made of transparent plastic is the key to this stability because the light travels through a consistent material. The light paths, which are divergent, are then bounced off a slanted surface at the base of the AM200 module 90 degrees going horizontally to the two spherical surfaces at the end of the optical block. The two spherical surfaces here act as separator lenses sending the light rays back to the CCD line sensor package.

At this point, one set of the rays goes to the upper CCD line sensor while the other goes to the lower CCD sensor (this is where the explanation gets dicey). The sensors receive the rays with each element of the CCD line sensor (each line containing 100 elements) reacting and outputting electronic charges in response to the brightness of the subject. The electronic outputs from the upper line sensor and that of the lower line sensor are then transferred to the AF Interface Integrated Circuit and then passed to the microcomputer unit which compares the two sensor lines output data. This detects the degree of focus of the image. The three bit microcomputer uses the special autofocus software to quickly process the focus information gathered from the 200 CCD sensors. It is this software that ensures fast, responsive AF operation.

At the same time, information is being transmitted from the lens to the camera body via the lens' microcomputer to the camera's microcomputer. Analysis of the light from the AM200 is transmitted to the AF Motor Control Integrated Circuit which takes all the input and translates the data to drive the coreless autofocus motor. The motor receives signals instructing it in which direction to turn and how fast to turn. This then turns the lens to focus the image on the film plane creating an in-focus photograph. The final procedure is an encoder that monitors motor movement to assure precise braking operation, preventing the lens from focusing beyond the subject. What took pages to explain, in reality happens at the speed of light. A truly amazing process occuring in the palm of your hand!

The Coreless Motor

This dialog skims over a strategic part of the Nikon autofocus system, the "coreless" motor. A big part of the speed of this process is the coreless motor which actually drives the lens elements. Uniquely Nikon, the coreless motor is missing the typical wire wrapped central coiled axis which requires a larger physical space and inertia to rotate. The coreless motor operates with only a cylindrical coil which requires less inertia to move. Basically, a large magnet responding to electrical impulses moves in an air gap. The magnet is wrapped around a shaft which connects to the lens drive gear focusing the lens when told to do so. This design provides a higher torque, quicker acceleration and higher accuracy because it offers stepless rotation. It is this coreless motor that allows Nikon to keep its promise of retaining its bayonet F lens mount. The power and smaller size of the coreless motor avoids having to use a larger lens mount to provide room for it to operate. It is this type of thinking and technology that makes Nikon autofocus such an excellent and reliable tool for photographers.

One of the updates in the N8008s is the changing of this motor. The coreless motor of the N8008 was replaced in the N8008s with the coreless motor used in the F4. A faster motor with more torque, the F4 motor provides the N8008s with faster response and focusing speed. The optical block, CCD sensors and software though is the same in the N8008s as in the N8008.

The Critical Element in the Formula

It is important to remember that as the photographer, you have the final say as to a photograph's content. In that pursuit, it's imperative that you remember that the camera is deriving all of its autofocus information from those tiny brackets in the center of the viewfinder screen. Autofocus requires that your subject be centered in the frame. This is quite often not the most pleasing composition. And there are conditions in which the camera will not be able to use autofocus because of where those brackets are in relation to the subject. There are ways to have it focus on a subject and then recompose and solve some of the other autofocus problems which will be discussed later.

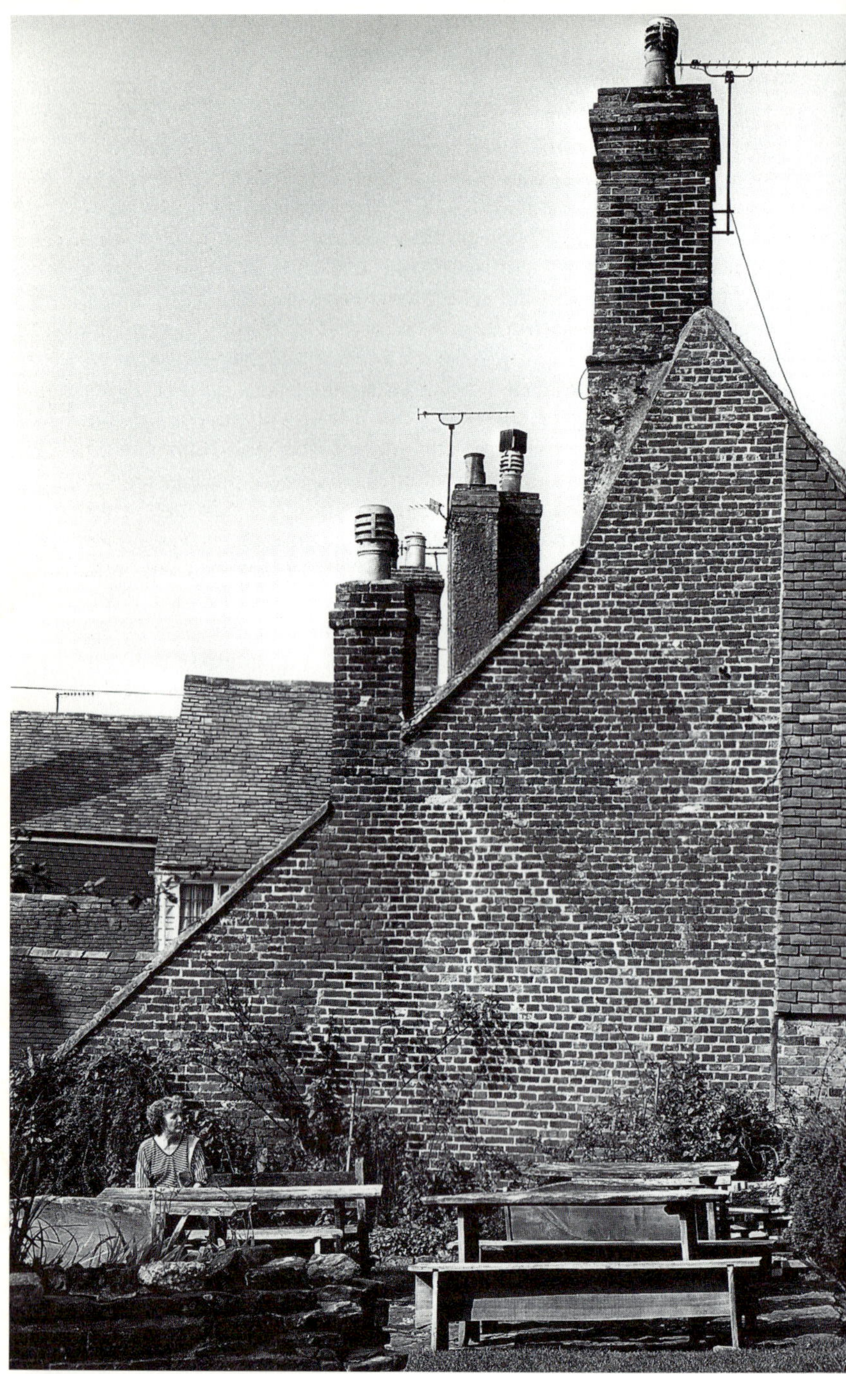

Using Autofocus

Making the most of the system requires not just understanding how to turn it on, but also how to use it for greatest effect. Let's start with the basics, operation of the camera. All autofocus operations require autofocus lenses. All Nikkor autofocus lenses except AF-I lenses will operate on the N8008s in all modes. Some autofocus lenses have on their barrel a separate switch which must be set for the lens to focus automatically. Doing this puts less strain on the entire system and speeds up operation.

Engaging the autofocus mode requires switching the lever located on the front of the body under the lens release button. This is a three station switch with detents and markings of "M", "S", and "C". "M" stands for manual focus in which you, the photographer are in control of focusing the lens. "S" stands for Single Servo Autofocus Mode and "C" stands for Continuous Servo Autofocus Mode. It is the "S" and "C" modes that we're interested in for the moment.

Single Servo Autofocus

By switching the camera to the "S" mode, you've activated the single servo autofocus. In this mode, the camera will not fire unless the subject is in focus! To activate the system, turn on the camera and partially depress the shutter release button. The camera's autofocus system should jump alive with the whirl of the motor as it focuses the lens. With the subject in the center, the camera should instantly lock onto it. (There are conditions in which the AF system will not function which will be covered shortly.) If this is the photograph desired, pressing the shutter release all the way down will capture the in focus subject on film.

What if the composition created by placing the subject dead center is not desired? With the autofocus system locked on the subject and while still depressing the shutter release, the subject can be reframed by redirecting the camera. This must be done

By using the autofocus lock feature, a photographer is able to focus on an off-center subject and then recompose the image.

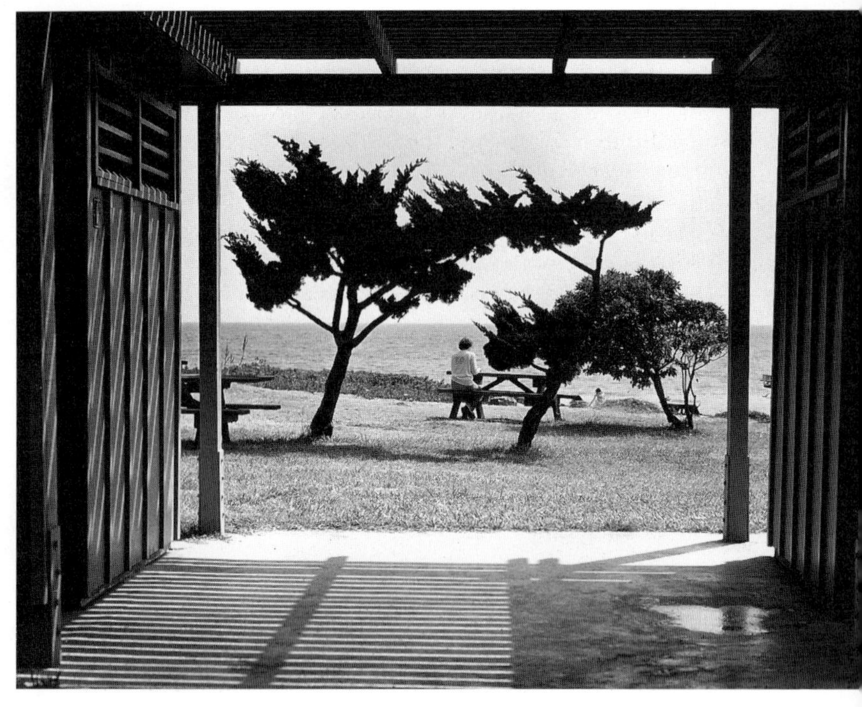

Using autofocus with this scene was easy because the subject was centrally located within the viewfinder's autofocus brackets.

with care, changing the distance between the camera and subject will alter the focus. Depressing the shutter release button completely will fire the camera. If the camera is in the "S" film advance mode, the camera will take just one frame. Be forewarned that each time you let your finger up to fire again, the camera will refocus. If the subject is not in the center of the brackets, the camera will refocus on whatever is there. This could cost you precious photographs.

If the camera is in either the "CL" or "CH" film advance mode, the camera will fire multiple frames until the shutter release button is no longer depressed. As long as the subject stays in the AF brackets, the camera will take in-focus photographs frame after frame. If you focus on the subject and then recompose the photograph by moving the subject out of the AF brackets, all shots after graph by moving the subject out of the AF brackets, all shots after the first one will be out of focus. The reason is after the first image, the system will refocus. With the subject no longer in the AF brackets, the camera will focus on something else. When recomposing, beware that all you'll get is one in-focus frame from this film advance mode.

Nikon has made it possible for you to have your cake and eat it, too. Below the depth-of-field preview button at the base of the lens mount is the AF-L or Autofocus Lock button. This button prevents the camera from refocusing. It can be used in either "S" or "C" mode and solves our just mentioned problem. With the film advance mode set to either "CL" or "CH", the autofocus set to "S", the camera's autofocus can lock onto the subject and then the photograph can be recomposed. At this point depress the AF-L button and fire off as many frames as desired. The autofocus will be locked into place for each exposure preventing it from refocusing after the first frame. Releasing the AF-L button puts everything back to normal.

Continuous Servo Autofocus

Switching the autofocus lever to "C", engages the Continuous Servo Autofocus mode. In this mode, the autofocus system will continually search for a subject to focus on as long as the shutter

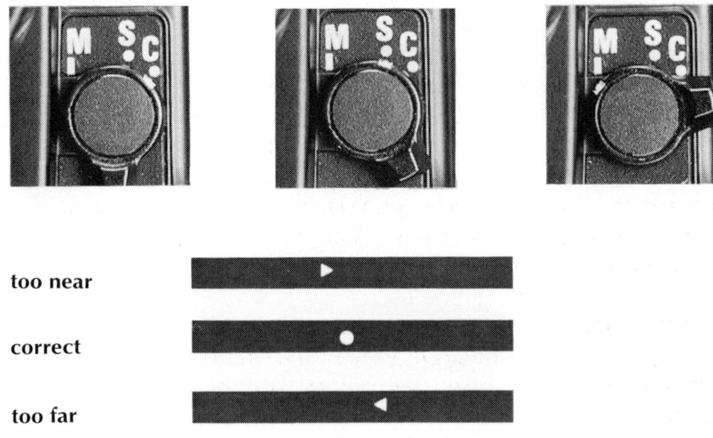

Viewfinder Autofocus Indicators

release is lightly depressed. It will lock on a subject, but if the camera is moved or the subject should move, the camera will refocus. The difference between this and the "S" mode is "S" will not refocus unless the shutter release is released and then depressed again. And in this mode, the camera will fire whether the subject is in-focus or not.

The "C" autofocus mode can be used with any of the three film advance modes, but it works best for shooting moving subjects in one of the continuous film advance modes. In "C" autofocus mode, you want to be able to take advantage of the fast response time of the camera.

An upgrade included in the N8008s involves the "C" autofocus mode. With the autofocus set to "C" and the Film Advance set to "CL", focus tracking is in operation. Focus tracking, in essence, computes and adjusts for subject movement while the camera is being fired.

The camera's computer analyzes the speed of the moving subject, its distance as it travels from the camera and its relationship to focus detection data. It then uses these calculations to make split-second changes in the focus. These changes are made in the last microseconds before the camera shutter is fired.

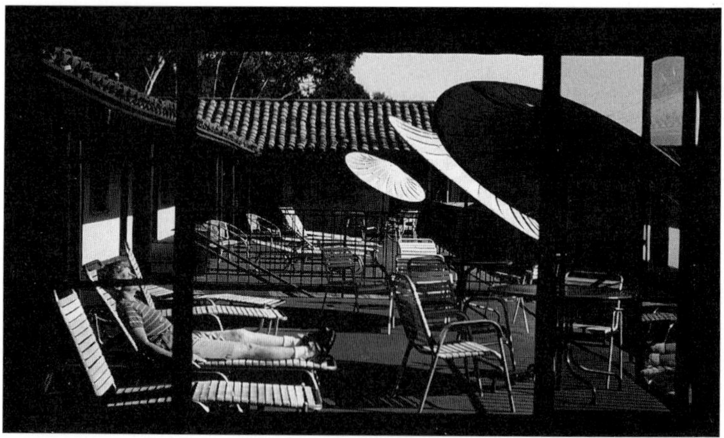

Glass can confuse the autofocus sensor, thus, it's recommended that you use manual focus when shooting subjects such as this.

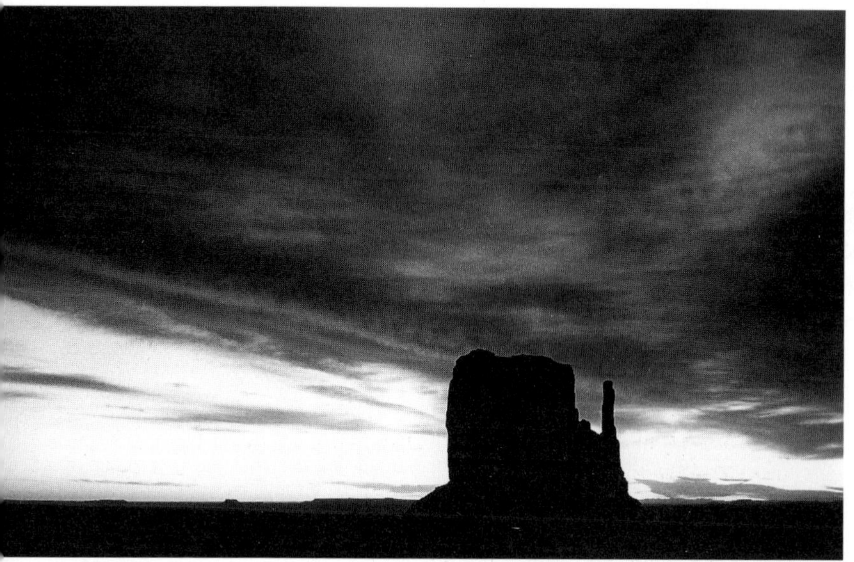

In this scene the "S" or single servo autofocus mode was used. Since the subject was not in the center of the scene, autofocus was locked on the subject, then the picture was reframed with the shutter release partially depressed.

Which mode to select when: A general rule of thumb is the "S" mode is for stationary subjects and the "C" is for moving subjects. Subjects such as scenics, portraits or any other non or slow moving object are great for "S". The insurance provided by "S" mode of not firing unless the subject is sharp is also nice. But what if your portrait subject is a small child? "S" might not be the right choice, because children usually don't hold still.

In this case or when photographing any subjects which constantly move, such as sports or wildlife, "C" is the best option. In fact, continuous autofocus mode will often be the most successful way to capture otherwise difficult photographic subjects. Remember, the "C" mode allows you to achieve the same focus lock by using the AF-L button. Picking the right mode also depends on the subject and the system's reaction to it.

Autofocus Viewfinder Information

On the left of the viewfinder, signals concerning autofocus operation are displayed. These signals appear whether the camera is being used in autofocus or manual focus mode. An "X" appears when the subject is of insufficient contrast or brightness for the camera to read. A right or left pointing arrow appears to indicate which direction to turn the focusing ring. A solid black dot will appear when the subject is sharp.

When focus tracking is activated and the image is sharp, both of the arrows will light. The normal solid black dot does not appear in this mode, just the two arrows which indicate that the subject is in focus.

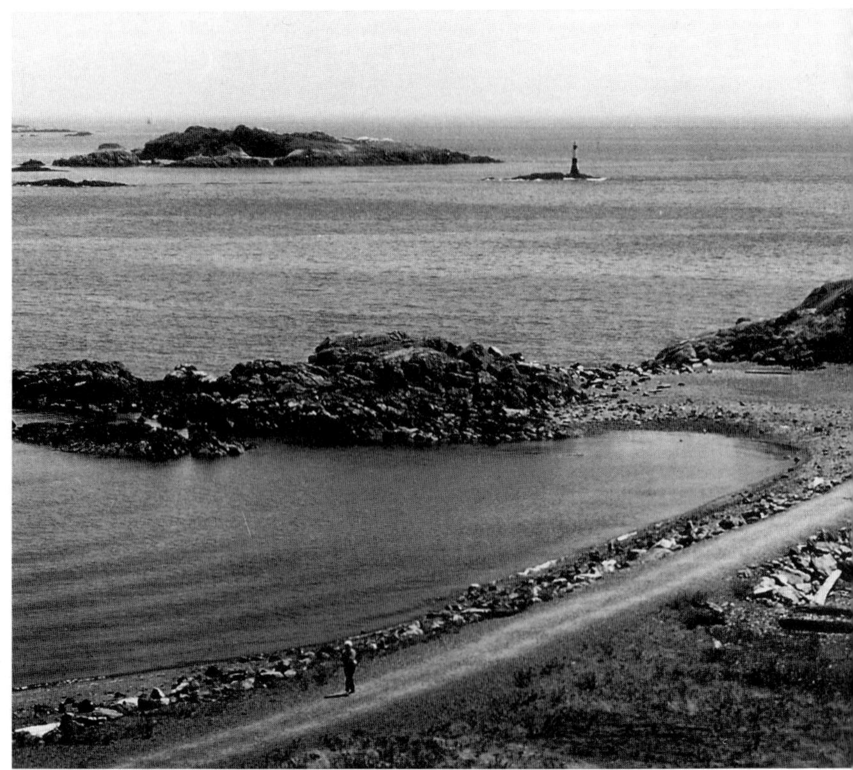

When Not To Use Autofocus

As mentioned before, the autofocus sensors depend on brightness to operate accurately. In conditions which are dark (the system functions down to -1 EV) or low contrast, there may not be enough brightness for the camera to focus. You'll quickly know when these situations occur as the lens will search back and forth, back and forth, to find the subject. In these conditions, switching to manual focus is recommended or necessary.

Your basic snapshot will be easily handled by autofocus, but the extremely creative or technical shots will not. The system really loves strong vertical or diagonal lines. These are often

Matrix metering produced perfect exposure of this British Columbia seascape.

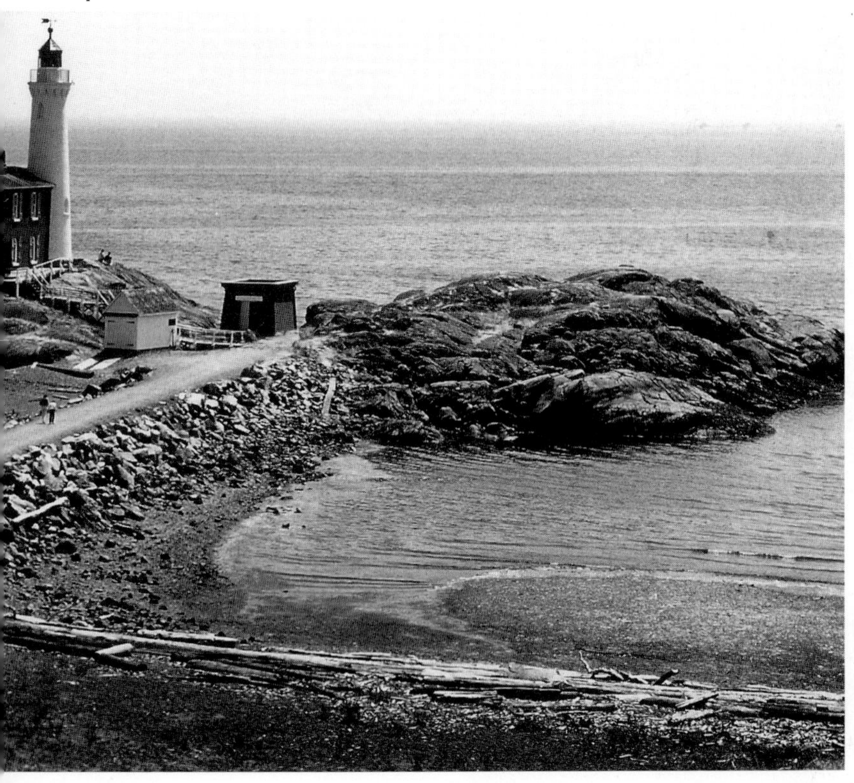

found in areas behind or in front of a subject, things such as furniture, branches, buildings, fences, etc.

Other situations where the autofocus should be "ignored" are bright subjects with a shiny surface, strongly backlit scenes or several subjects located at different distances. Also, if the photographer is trying to shoot discreetly, autofocus should not be used. Although not excessively noisy, autofocus does make more sound than manually focusing the lens.

The biggest reason for not using autofocus is the subject and how the photographer wants to capture it. At times it may be quicker to focus manually and shoot rather than center the subject in the autofocus brackets and then recompose the image. Macro is another good example of a situation in which autofocus is not the best choice. The system tends to have difficulty with the lighting and contrast conditions associated with macro. These are times when switching to manual focus is the best option.

Autofocus In Low Light

In those situations where the light or contrast level is too low for the autofocus to work, the AF illuminator on Nikon flash units can help. With the autofocus set to the "S" mode, the AF illuminator on the SB-20, SB-22, SB-23, SB-24 and SB-25 will emit a red beam in which the autofocus sensor can lock onto and focus the camera. The beam will only stay on for the length of time that is required to focus. This opens up a whole new world of photography that was only available previously with the painful "flashlight held between the knees" method. This will not work with moving subjects as you are operating in the "S" mode.

Manual Focus Mode

The bright, high-eyepoint finder of the N8008s is a natural for manual focusing. Switching the focus mode selector (and the manual/auto switch found on some lenses) to "M" is all that is required to disengage the autofocus. In situations such as those mentioned above, manual focus may be a must. But on many occasions, it's simply more fun and efficient to focus manually.

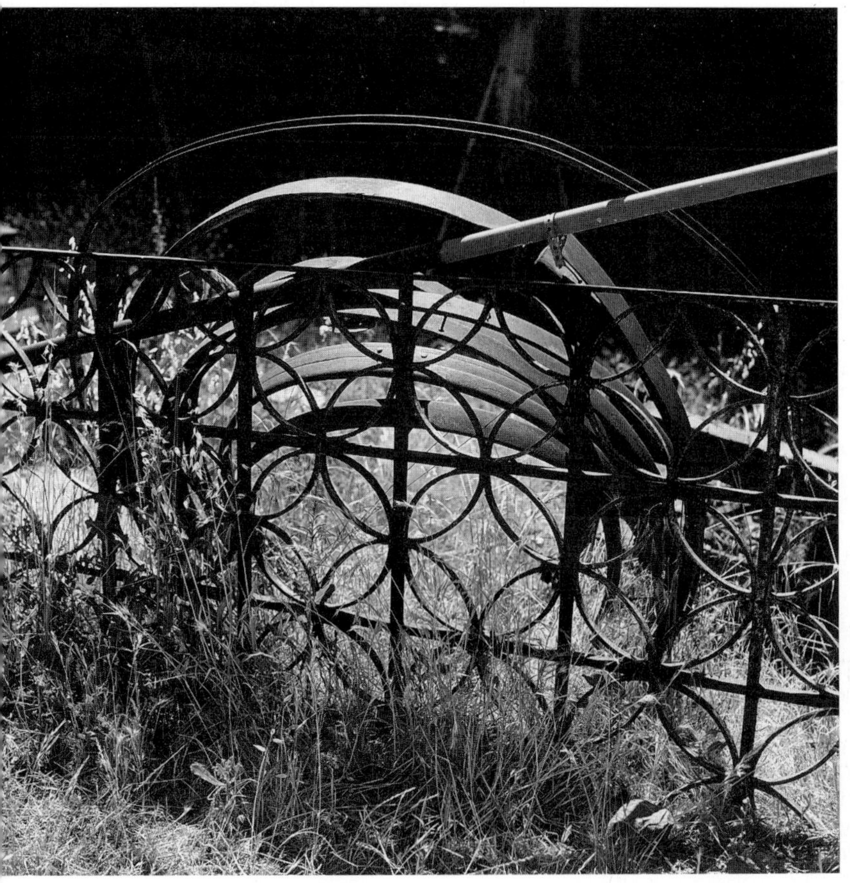

Manual focus is recommended for photographing scenes with several layers, such as those shot through a fence or window. The autofocus system may have trouble choosing between whether to focus on the foreground or background.

The N8008s is equipped with Nikon's Type B Focusing Screen. It is an excellent general use screen with a Matte/Fresnel field on which the image is focused. 5mm and 12mm references circles and the AF brackets are centered on the screen.

Sharp focus is achieved by simply looking at the image in the viewfinder and turning the focusing ring on the lens until the sul ject looks sharp. This can be difficult with some subjects or in low light conditions. Photographers who are not proficient at manually focusing may have a hard time seeing when the subject is in-focus. The electronic rangefinder in the N8008s offers manual focus assist.

Part of the autofocus system, the electronic rangefinder operates by providing a solid black dot in the viewfinder display when the subject is in focus. There are two arrows or triangles in the bottom left of the viewfinder. If the subject is not in focus, either the left or right arrow will be present. This indicates the direction in which the lens should be focused to get the subject in focus. This is part of the electronic rangefinder. Remember that this only works when the subject is located dead center in the autofocus brackets.

In the "M" mode, the camera can be focused on the subject until the black dot appears, and then recomposed moving the subject out of dead center. In doing this, the solid black dot will disappear as the brackets are no longer on the subject. Don't let this alarm you, just be prepared for it.

Additional Autofocus Assist

A freeze focus feature is available when the MF-21 Multi-Control Back is attached to the N8008s. Connecting up with the autofocus software, the camera waits for a subject to appear in the autofocus brackets and then takes the photograph automatically. An MC-12A Motor Remote Trigger Release is required, allowing the shutter release to be depressed the entire time while waiting for the subject. Extreme precision in setting it up is also required, as the bracket is so small and the CCD sensors so sensitive. The subject must break the prefocused distance just right, be within the autofocus bracket and be of the right contrast and brightness for the camera to fire. Experimentation and practice are required to get the most out of this option and make it productive.

The N8008s Metering Systems

The N8008 has two metering methods, the N8008s has three. Common to both are matrix and center-weighted metering, and unique to the N8008s is spot metering. Both center-weighted and spot metering systems are usually used for finding the correct exposure value in technically difficult situations. Because they often cause more problems than they solve for the basic photographer, they are rarely used. These problems come from the lack of understanding by most photographers of how the meter interprets what it sees and calculates exposure.

Matrix Metering

How it works?: The image is divided up into five segments, roughly the same size as each other with one in the center and the other four in corresponding corners. The actual sensor, a one-component SPD sensor module with five segments for precise alignment, is located in the prism head of the camera. Each segment's reading is compared against two basic parameters, its brightness value and degree of contrast. This is then segmented into sets of brightness and contrast classifications that together comprise a 5 x 5 matrix. (Now we know where the term matrix metering comes from.) It must be kept in mind that a powerful inboard computer is doing all these computations. This computer relies on Nikon's own advanced software which contains over 100,000 brightness and contrast range combinations on which to base its exposure advice.

With these values in the system, the computer compares the segments to determine which of the five is brightest and by how much, which is darkest and by how much. From this, the matrix system assigns a suitable algorithmic pattern from four computation methods: low-brightness weighted, high-brightness weighted, average and center segment. It selects which of these methods best fits the situation being read by the sensor, takes that information and then bases its advice of shutter speed and aperture for the best exposure.

It boils down to this, the N8008s matrix meter can be trusted in about 90% of the situations typically found in photography!

These computations are happening at the speed of light and on a continual basis when the camera is turned on. This amazing system which was suspect when first introduced is now the industry standard.

Note: *Only lenses with a CPU (autofocus and "P" lenses) will work on the N8008s in matrix mode. If in matrix mode and a non CPU lens is attached to the camera, the camera will automatically revert to center-weighted metering.*

Center-weighted Metering

By depressing the metering system selection button on the left of the prism and turning the command input control dial, the metering pattern can be set. The symbol in the LCD panel will be the only indication of the switch in metering pattern. The symbol for center-weighted metering is a dot surrounded by two parenthesis. The center-weighted metering system bases 75% of its metering advice on the large circle seen on the screen through the viewfinder. The remaining screen area contributes only 25% of the information. In practical terms, the meter pays attention to the element that fills the center of the screen and places three times as much emphasis on it for calculating exposure.

Spot Metering

Depressing the metering system selection button and turning the command input control dial again on the N8008s, switches the system to spot metering, represented by a dot on the LCD panel. The Spot Meter can be thought of as a super sensitive, center-weighted meter. It calculates exposure from the 3.5mm circle that immediately surrounds the autofocus brackets. The spot meter does not look at any other part of the screen, deriving 100% of its advice from that center spot. Spot metering is not a system for the average shooter; it requires an immense understanding of exposure, exposure range and film latitude.

What The Meter Is Saying

The meter does nothing more than provide the photographer with advice. It is up to the photographer to either accept that advice and shoot or change it in some manner. Knowing when to accept the advice and when not to takes experience. Meters base their exposure on the assumption that a scene is composed of an equal number of dark and light areas which average out to be middle or 18% gray. This is typically described by saying that a camera meter when exposing a white wall or a black wall wants the wall to be gray in the final photograph.

The way one knows when the camera meter is being fooled is understanding basic lighting. This depends on the meter that resides in your head! To figure exposure in full sun, convert the ISO of the film being used to the most similar shutter speed possible and combine that with an aperture of f/16. For example, ISO 100 film would convert to a shutter speed of 1/125. This number or any combination equaling the same exposure value (i.e. 1/1000 at f/5.6 or 1/250 at f/11) is the correct exposure for any scene in full sun. Going back to that white wall, the camera meter may advise an exposure of 1/250 at f/16 which would underexpose the photograph, causing the wall to appear gray. Using this basic daylight rule would produce a better exposure. Experience is still one of the best ways of knowing when the camera meter is being fooled.

Overriding the Meter

The N8008s has exposure compensation. This permits overriding and biasing the metering system by a predetermined amount. It equally affects all metering and exposure modes. It provides a ten stop range of compensation in 1/3 stop increments, from underexposure (minus) by five stops to overexposure (plus) of five stops.

Setting the exposure compensation requires pressing the exposure compensation button next to the power switch on top of the camera and turning the command input control dial. The "+/-" symbol will appear on the LCD panel and in the viewfinder to remind you that exposure compensation has been set. Turning the control dial in either one direction or the other will change the value to either plus or minus. An analog scale will appear to indicate the dialed in plus or minus compensation up to two stop. A digital number will appear, counting off the same compensation up to five stops. But this number does not show plus or minus compensation which must be confirmed by looking at the analog scale.

In situations, such as snow scenes where you desire to make the snow all white (remember the 18% gray value), an overexposure compensation of one or more stops should be dialed in. This will bias the meter so the snow is rendered white. Exposure compensation can be vital in many photographic situations but requires not only technical knowledge of its effect on exposure and subject detail, but knowledge of how it will affect what you're communicating about the scene.

Note: *The meter sensor resides in the prism head not far from the eyepiece. If your eye is not up against the eyepiece, extraneous light can get in, confusing the meter and altering the exposure by as much as two stops. Whenever you are not viewing through the camera while in any mode other than manual, always use the eyepiece shield (DK-8) that comes with the camera.*

Flash Metering

The N8008s features TTL (Through-The-Lens) flash metering. This should not be confused with the ambient light metering systems just discussed. The TTL flash metering system is separate from the other metering modes as far as reading the light. The TTL sensor for flash is in the base of the mirror box, right next to the AF sensor. It is center-weighted, no matter what metering mode is selected for the ambient light.

Auto Exposure Modes

The N8008s has a well-rounded complement of six different exposure modes. These modes provide the photographer with a complete range of cameras from a totally automated "point and shot" to a totally manual camera with every option in between. Which mode is right for you depends on your style of photography and level of expertise. It also depends on how fast the action is and if you want the camera to take some of the work off your shoulders.

It may also depend on your equipment, as not all Nikkor lenses will afford you the availability of all modes. The Program modes and Shutter Speed Priority will only work with lenses with a CPU. This group is comprised of autofocus and "P" lenses. In these modes, if a a non-CPU lens is attached to the camera, the camera will automatically switch to aperture priority mode as well as to center-weighted metering. See page 145.

Selecting an exposure mode simply requires pressing down the "Mode" button on the left of the camera and then turning the command input control dial. On the LCD panel in a small box in the top left corner, the appropriate letter will appear for each mode. These are "PD" for Dual Program, "PH" for High-speed Program, "P" for Program, "S" for Shutter Priority, "A" for Aperture Priority and "M" for Manual. In the viewfinder, the same letters will appear, except "P" represents all Program modes rather than three different symbols.

Program Exposure Modes

There are three program modes available in the N8008s, Dual Program (PD), High-speed Program (PH) and Program (P). Each mode has its own unique properties making them all valuable tools. Each program mode requires the lens on the camera be set to its minimum f/stop. Most of the time, this is f/22 or f/32. To prevent the accidental moving of the aperture ring off the minimum f/stop, Nikkor autofocus lenses come with an aperture lock. If the minimum aperture is not set, the letters "FEE" will appear in the LCD panel as well as in the viewfinder.

The program modes select and set the shutter speed and aperture that will produce correct exposure. The shutter speed and aperture selected are based on advice from the meter and the program mode in use. With any of the program modes, the shutter speed and aperture are stepless. What this means is there are no defined settings, allowing the camera to select shutter speeds such as 1/21, 1/269, 1/532 and apertures of f/7, f/9.3 or f/14 . This presents an unequaled ability to fine tune the exposure.

A "Lo" or "HI" message will appear in the viewfinder and LCD panel when the light level is outside the range of the system. For example, if there is not enough illumination to make an exposure, "Lo" will appear. On the other hand, if the aperture is wide open on a sunny day, the "HI" message may appear. In the case of a "Lo" message, a flash might be the solution to the problem.

Program (P): This tends to provide the best combination for average photographic situations. The aperture will tend to be closed down in this mode to provide a little extra depth of field. The shutter speed will be correspondingly slower. An effective use for the "P" mode is to provide greater depth of field when using shorter lenses.

High-speed Program (PH): This will choose a higher shutter speed for the shutter speed/aperture combination. This mode is typically used in conjunction with telephoto lenses where a higher shutter speed is desired to minimize the effects of camera movement during the exposure. Higher shutter speeds require larger lens apertures creating less depth of field.

Dual Program (PD): In this mode, the camera switches automatically between the Normal Program or High-speed Program depending on the lens in use. With focal lengths of 135mm or shorter, the Normal Program (P) mode will be selected. With lenses or zooms set at 135mm or longer, the High-speed Program (PH) will be selected. This mode is extremely useful for action photography that involves frequent lens changes.

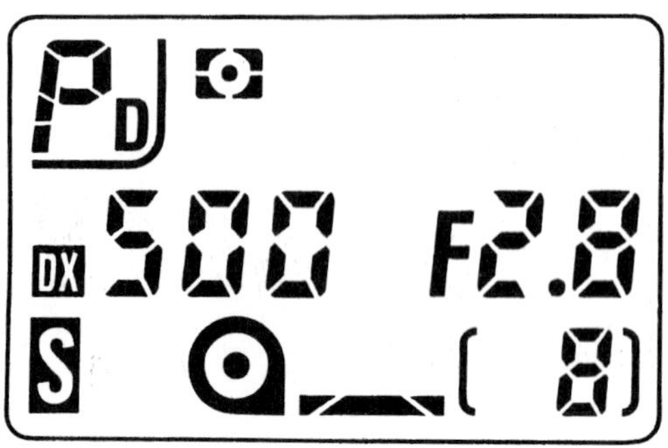

The N8008s' LCD panel showing Dual Program mode in use.

Flexible Program: All three of the Program exposure modes have a Flexible Program. This is a valuable feature that allows you to change the shutter speed/aperture combination if you so desire. The combination can be changed by turning the command input control dial in any direction within the limits of the f/stop of the lens. The "P" in the viewfinder and in the LCD panel will blink when it has been shifted from the advised combination. At any time, the camera's advised exposure settings can be reset by turning the command input control dial until the "P" no longer blinks. The Flexible Program will be automatically canceled once the camera shuts off after 8 seconds.

Flash Photography with Program Modes

Using a Nikon dedicated flash with the program modes makes flash photography simple. In any of these modes, the camera will automatically select the correct shutter speed between 1/60-1/250 (flash set to normal) or 30 seconds to 1/250 (flash set to rear). The camera will also set the aperture within a range of f/4 - f/16. The exception is in PH where the maximum usable aperture varies according to the film speed in use and minimum aperture of the lens. Read the *Magic Lantern Guide to Nikon SB-25* to learn more about using flash with the N8008s.

Shutter Priority Exposure Mode

Represented with an S on the LCD and in the viewfinder, this mode gives the photographer complete control over shutter speed, leaving the aperture selection up to the camera. The avail-

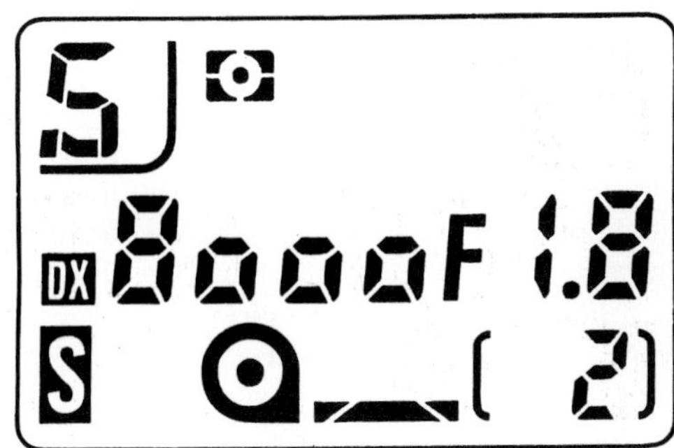

The N8008s' LCD panel showing Shutter Priority mode in use.

able shutter speeds start at 30 seconds and continue in one stop increments to 1/8000 second. They are set using the command input control dial. The camera will select the aperture for correct exposure based on the selected shutter speed. The apertures are stepless as previously discussed.

The lens must be set to its minimum aperture to operate in this mode. If the aperture should slip from this setting, the "FEE" message will appear in the viewfinder and on the LCD panel. The "HI" and "Lo" messages signal possible over- or underexposure as discussed in the previous section, "Program Exposure Modes." An analog scale will appear which will indicate in 1/3 stop increments how much the exposure is off. This scale has a two stop range, so if the exposure is greater than this, an arrow at the end of the scale indicates the light range is beyond the range of the scale.

When to Use Shutter Priority Mode: This mode is for those situations where a desired shutter speed is required to either stop action or convey motion. If photographing an air race, for example, a shutter speed of 1/500 second might be required to stop the action. The scene changes as the planes run the coarse and in Shutter Priority mode, the camera will change the aperture to make corrections in exposure. Or, to photograph running water as a blur, a slow shutter speed can be chosen. This mode will compensate for changing lighting conditions by adjusting the aperture.

Aperture Priority Exposure Mode

The best mode for the majority of photographers and photographic situations, Aperture Priority (A) provides the greatest means of creative control. In this mode, the photographer selects the aperture and the camera selects the correct shutter speed. The shutter speeds are stepless in this mode, providing the most accurate control over exposure. Unlike manually set shutter speeds, the lens aperture can be set by the photographer anywhere between the one stop designations. In combination with stepless shutter speeds, exposure control can be maximized and extended as much as possible. This allows as much as one stop greater control over exposure compared to using Manual mode to lock in shutter speed.

This mode also gives the photographer complete control over

The N8008s' LCD panel showing Aperture Priority mode in use.

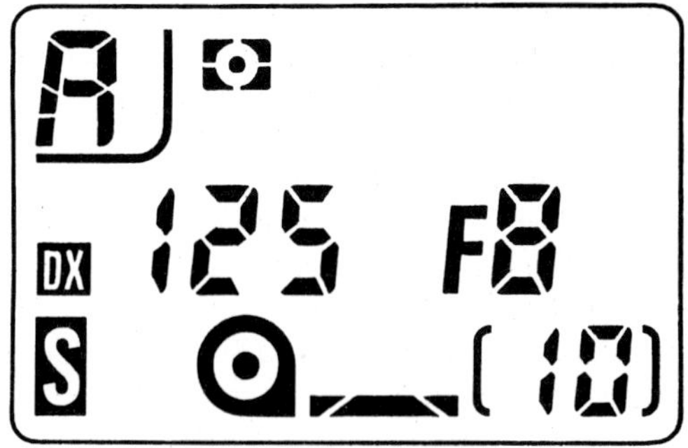

depth of field. This is very important as depth of field directly relates to how much of the subject and its surroundings will be in focus. This affects the way the subject is communicated to others through your photograph, and therefore, the success of your photographs.

Auto Exposure Lock

Many advanced photographers do not like using automatic exposure modes. Their complaint is that the camera is in control of depth of field, shutter speed and exposure. This is simply not true. The photographer is always in control even in these modes! No matter which mode is used, it is up to the photographer to analyze the advice provided by the camera. Remember the basic daylight rule from the section "What the Meter Is Saying".

If the camera meter has been fooled, the photographer can override it without changing the selected mode. Just point the camera off the subject to take the exposure reading. For example, meter off a gray card or a mid-tone object in the scene rather than a very dark or light subject. When the desired shutter speed, aperture or combination of both, appears in the viewfinder/LCD panel, slide over the AE-L (auto-exposure lock) button towards the eyepiece. (AE-L button is located just right of the eyepiece on the back of the camera.) This locks in the exposure selected by you, the photographer, overriding the advice of the camera. Then simply recompose and capture the photograph. Releasing the AE-L button cancels its lock on the exposure and everything goes back to normal.

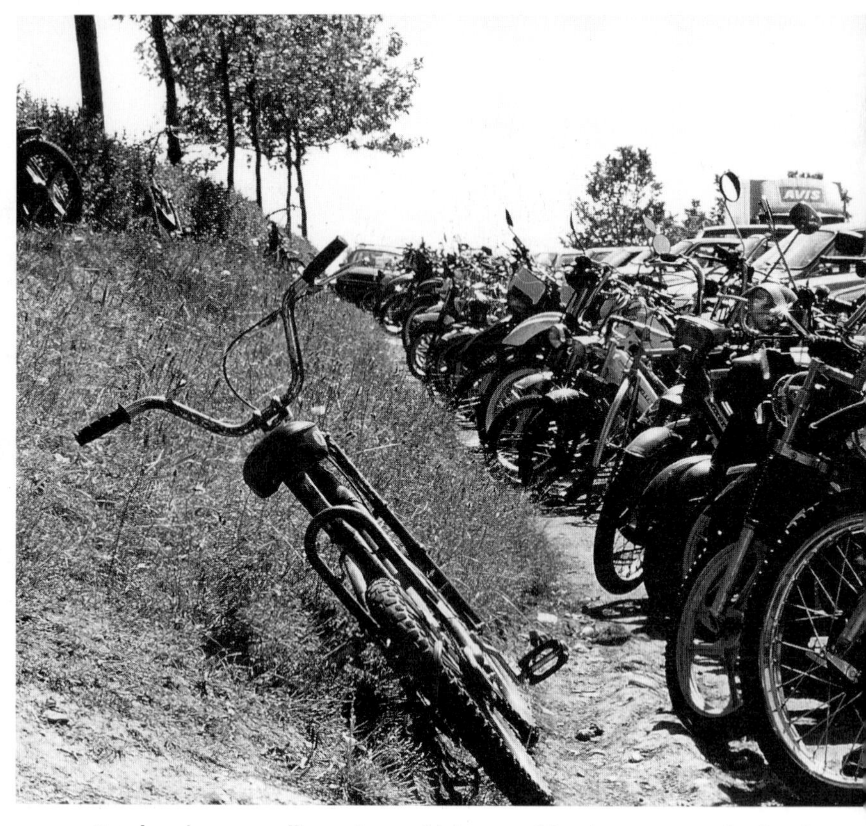

By choosing a small aperture which gave this picture great depth of field, the photographer emphasized the number of motorcycles parked here.

Additional Overrides

Do you have other options in overriding the advice of the camera? Yes, you can switch to manual mode and dial in any shutter speed and aperture combination. Or you can depress the exposure compensation button and dial in compensation. All these methods require you take your attention away from the subject temporarily, but the AE-L solution requires the least amount of lost time focusing on the subject. It also requires the least amount of time to reset everything back to normal. You need to find the method that best works for you.

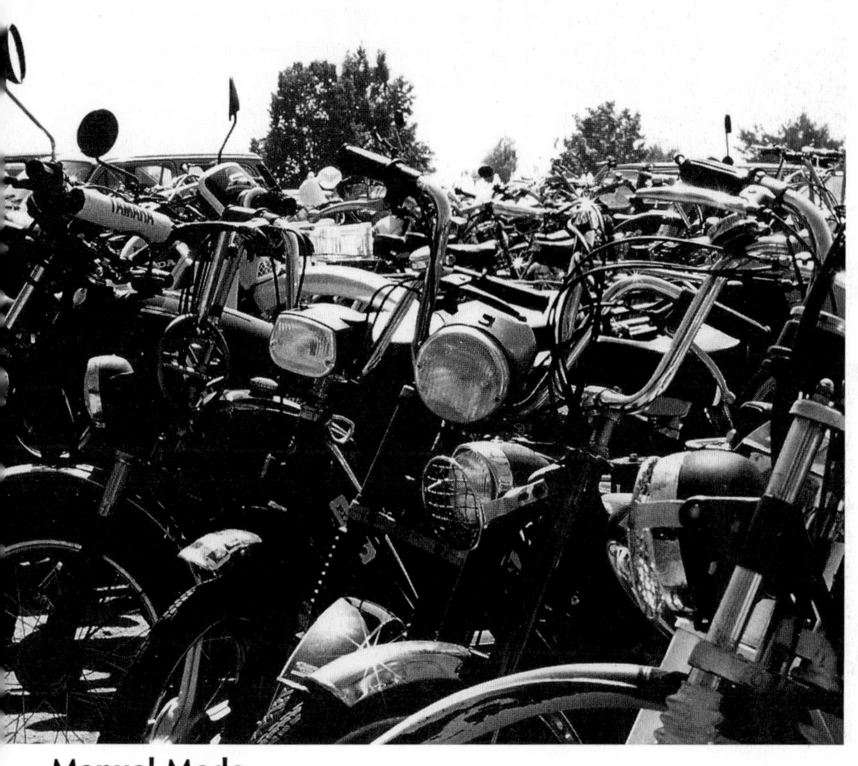

Manual Mode

Manual mode (M) puts exposure control completely in the hands of the photographer. In this mode, the photographer must dial in the shutter speed and aperture to achieve correct exposure. The correct shutter speed and aperture setting can be determined by using any of the three TTL camera metering systems, or a hand held meter.

In this mode, an analog scale appears in the viewfinder and on the LCD panel. The selected shutter speed and f/stop also appear in both locales. With a non-CPU lens, the aperture will not appear, only the shutter speed. The lens can still be used. Also see, page 145. The analog scale will display over, correct or

The N8008s' LCD panel showing Manual mode in use.

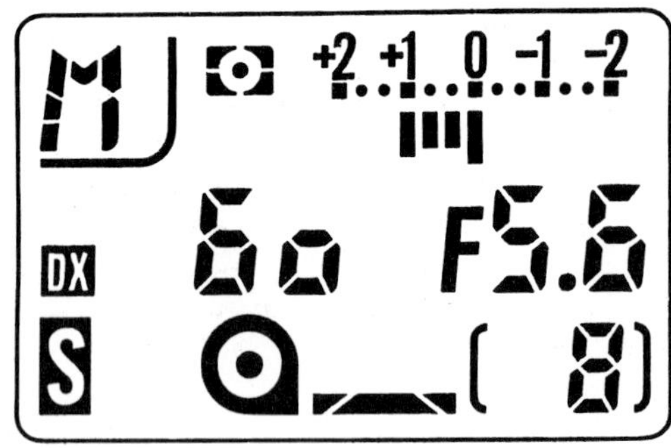

underexposure based on the shutter speed and aperture selected. Overexposure is indicated on the "+" side of the analog scale in 1/3 stops increments up to two stops. Underexposure is shown in the same way but on the "-" side of the scale. Correct exposure is represented when a single line is aligned with the "0" and no other lines appear on either side.

Changing the reading on the meter's scale requires changing either the shutter speed or aperture. Shutter speeds are selected by turning the command input control dial in either direction until the desired shutter speed appears. The aperture is changed by turning the aperture ring on the lens itself. In either case, the camera meter can be fooled to give an incorrect exposure just as in any other mode. In manual mode, the photographer can simply change the shutter speed, aperture or exposure compensation to make the needed adjustments.

In Manual Mode, shutter speeds of 30 seconds to 1/8000 are possible. There is also a "bulb" setting, in which the shutter remains open as long as the shutter release button is depressed. (It's best to use the MC-12A cord as it has a lock for long exposures unless you want to exercise your finger.) In this mode, the camera's meter does not provide exposure readings. Also, the camera remains on during the entire exposure using up battery power.

Using the "bulb" setting: In any exposure mode, if the LCD reads "Lo" and the shutter speed is past the 30 second mark, it is time to use the "bulb" setting. (Flash is another option.) Since the meter will not function when set at "bulb", how do you calculate exposure? First, change the film speed setting in one stop increments by doubling the ISO, for example, going from 100 to 200 and then to 400, etc. until the meter registers correct exposure. Then count how many stops were required to make the meter respond. Reset the correct film speed, set the exposure mode to Manual, and dial in the "bulb" setting. The duration of time that the shutter stays open must then be doubled for each stop counted. For example, if it took four stops for the meter to register correct exposure, the shutter speed increases from 30 seconds to 60 (1 stop), 120 (2 stops), 240 (3 stops) and finally to the right exposure of 480 seconds. Other problems might be encountered, but this will get your exposure in the ball park.

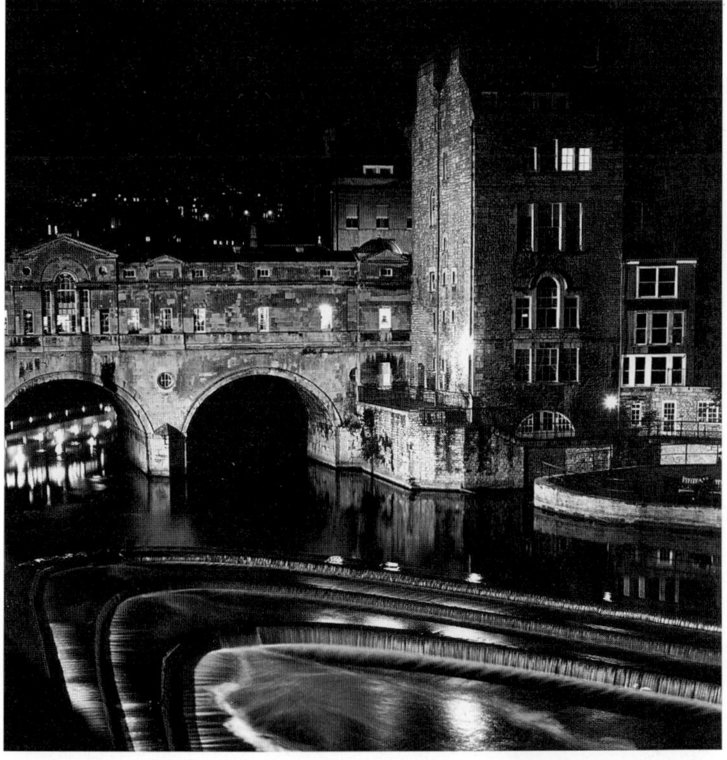

Time exposures, like this Bath, England scene, are easy and rewarding. Using ISO 100 film and an aperture of f/8, the photographer tried exposure times of 8, 14, and 20 seconds.

Nikon Flash Photography

Basic Principles

By using Nikon's sophisticated autoflash system, anyone can take flash pictures without time-consuming computations. Nevertheless, when using flash for creative photography most photographers find that it is still beneficial to understand how flash works. Thus, included in this chapter is a brief section on flash fundamentals. For those wishing to know even more about the Nikon Flash System and advanced flash technique, I recommend picking up a copy of the *Magic Lantern Guide to Nikon SB-25.*

Light Output, Duration and Distance

In flash photography, exposure is determined by the amount of light output by the flash unit, the duration of the light and the distance between the subject and the flash unit. The subject will receive less light the farther it is located from the source of the light. Light from a flash unit is subject to the Inverse Square Law which states that brightness decreases in proportion to the square of the distance.

Increased Light and Distance

Doubling the light increases the shooting range by slightly less than 1-1/2 times. Therefore, if the flash provides correct exposure for a subject 10 feet away with the camera's lens set at an aperture of f/5.6, opening the lens one full stop to f/4 will provide correct exposure only as far as 14 feet, not 20 feet. Opening the aperture one stop allows twice as much light to pass, but the flash will only reach only 1.4 times as far. Again, this is determined by the principle of the Inverse Square Law.

Guide Number

A guide number quantifies the relationship between brightness, distance, and film sensitivity and assists in calculating aperture and distance values in practical applications. Guide numbers are usually stated using ISO 100 film as the standard. While these calculations are generally unnecessary with today's automatic flash equipment, they sometimes are used in situations where manual adjustments to the flash output are required. Even when using a camera with through-the-lens (TTL) flash metering, flash exposure compensation may occasionally be necessary.

Guide numbers follow a logarithmic progression comparable to f/stops. (A numerically larger guide number means more light, while a numerically larger f/stop means less light.) For example, if the distance from the subject along with the guide number corresponding to the film sensitivity are known, the required aperture may be easily determined. This answers the question of what aperture to select to obtain the correct exposure for a subject at a given distance. Aperture = guide number/distance.

Note: *In the United States, guide numbers are expressed in feet and are consequently 3.3 times larger than corresponding metric guide numbers.*

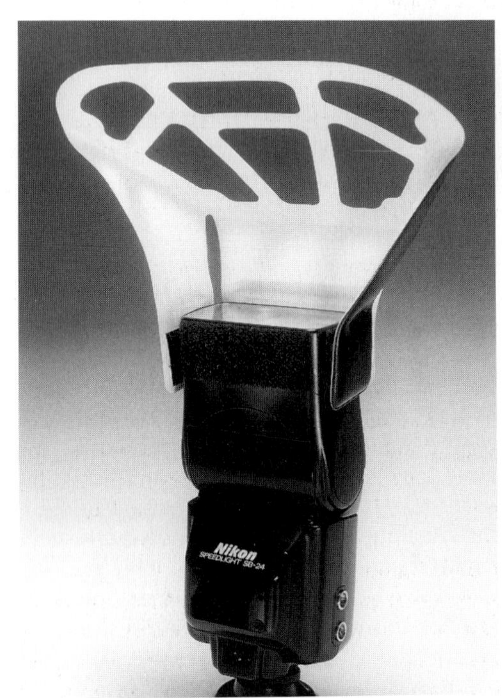

Reflectors and diffusers, like the Lumiquest Promax 80-20 shown here, are excellent for photographing people. They soften the light from the flash to reduce harsh shadows and create lighting that looks more natural.

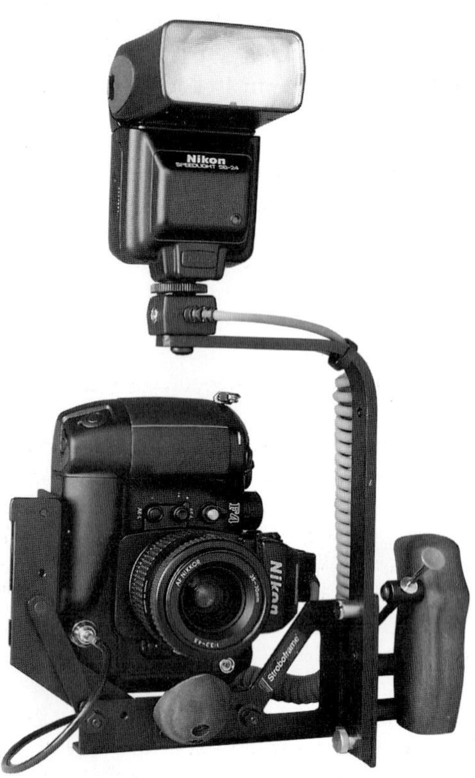

The Stroboframe RL-2000 is an excellent flash bracket to use with a Nikon camera and flash set-up.

Guide Numbers with Zoom Flash Heads

Typically, guide numbers are based on the image angle of a normal (50mm) lens. However, the guide number will change if the flash unit's angle of illumination is changed. With zoom flash heads such as on the Nikon SB-24 and SB-25 flash units, the angle of illumination is modified to cover the angle of view of different focal length lenses. This is accomplished by changing the position of the flash head diffuser in relation to the flash tube. By adjusting the zoom head, the flash energy is either concentrated on a smaller angle of illumination, which covers a longer distance, or diffused over a larger angle that covers a shorter distance. The smaller the angle of illumination (long focal length lenses), the greater the guide number; the greater the angle of illumination (short focal length lenses), the smaller the guide number. This explains why a flash unit - even though it always emits the same quantity of light - will have several different guide numbers when the zoom head is adjusted to cover different angles.

Color Temperature

The light from most flash units has a color temperature of 5600°K which approximates daylight. Thus, daylight-balanced film should be used for flash photography. Since it is similar to daylight, flash is an excellent source of light for augmenting natural light in fill flash photography.

Red-eye

Red-eye often occurs when using an on-camera flash unit. When the flash axis and lens axis are almost the same, the light reflected off the red retina at the rear of the eye becomes visible. When there is a significant distance between the lens and flash axis, however, this red light is reflected out of the image area. Diffusing or bouncing the light from the flash is one solution, but it reduces the flash intensity. A better alternative is the use of a flash bracket, such as those manufactured by Stroboframe®. These brackets raise the flash high above the camera, effectively eliminating red-eye.

Flash Synchronization

For proper results, the electronic flash must fire when the focal plane shutter is completely open. This shutter consists of two curtains which move in sequence across the film. The first curtain opens, uncovering the film for exposure, and then the second curtain closes providing a light-tight cover over the film again. Exposure time is changed by releasing the second curtain either sooner or later. Thus, the fastest synchronization speed for electronic flash is the highest shutter speed at which the first curtain has completely uncovered the film and the second has not yet begun to close. The synchronization speed only indicates the highest possible shutter speed for a flash exposure. For the N6000 series the flash sync speed is 1/125 second, for the N8008s it is 1/250 second. These cameras also allow the photographer to set slower shutter speeds for use with flash.

If the focal plane shutter is set at a speed higher than the fastest synchronization speed only a portion of the normal image area is exposed. The remainder of the film area, which was still covered by the curtains during the flash, will be severely underexposed. Nikon N6000 series and N8008s cameras automatically prevent this error. They simply refuse to fire a flash at too high a speed, and automatically default to the highest possible synchronization speed.

Autoflash Modes

In order to understand the advantages and limitations of different autoflash modes the photographer should have a basic knowledge of how they operate.

Flash Output Control

If the automatic flash "knows" the distance from the main subject and the selected aperture before firing, it will simply adjust its output accordingly before firing. A flash with a guide number of 40, an aperture of f/8, and a distance from the subject of 12 feet would automatically be adjusted downward to a guide number of 32 and at 9 feet to a guide number of 24, etc.

Control of Duration by Reflected Light

Conventional automatic flash units have an integrated external photo sensor which measures the light reflected by the subject during exposure. The flash control is independent of the camera. The flash duration ranges between approximately 1/200 sec. and 1/50000 sec. (1/1000 sec. and 1/23000 sec. for the Nikon SB-25).

The Test Flash Feature

A test flash may be fired with most flash units including the SB-25 (without film exposure) by manually triggering the flash unit. However, a test flash is not appraised by the TTL metering system in the camera; it is only read by the sensor built into the flash unit. If the test indicator has a positive response the flash output will probably be sufficient for correct exposure.

Conventional TTL Autoflash

In TTL autoflash mode, measurements are made Through The Lens (TTL). The mirror flips up, the aperture closes down, the shutter curtain opens fully, and then the flash fires. While the shutter is open a flash metering cell in the lower portion of the shutter is open a flash metering cell in the lower portion of the mirror chamber measures the light reflected off the film. It controls the flash duration based on this measurement and cuts off the flash at the appropriate moment.

Compared with conventional automatic flash units, TTL flash measures the image angle of the subject accurately. Lens attachments or filters are also taken into consideration. In TTL flash mode the aperture set on the lens is of relatively no consequence because different apertures are automatically compensated for by the flash unit.

Limitations of Conventional TTL Flash

There are limitations to this system. One is that the transistor or thyristor used in controlling the flash unit's duration has an intrinsic switching time. If the required flash duration is shorter than this switching time, overexposed images will result. This may occur if the distance from the subject is very small and the selected aperture very large. In this case, TTL-controlled flash exposures may be overexposed.

Another problem occurs whenever the main subject does not fill the picture and the background is at quite a distance. This causes only a fraction of the light emitted by the flash to be reflected by the subject. The remainder of this light is lost in the background "next to" the subject. The TTL autoflash attempts to counteract this by prolonging the duration of the flash. The result is often overexposed main subjects, especially if they are all in the foreground.

Subjects with Unusual Reflectance

If a subject absorbs or reflects light in an unusual manner, the automatic flash exposure may not be accurate. This is because a flash is calibrated for a subject with average reflecting power or "medium gray". Naturally dark subjects, with low reflectance, will be overly lightened and reproduced unnaturally light. Conversely, very light subjects with high reflecting power will appear too dark in the final photo. The bride in white in front of the white wall will be too dark; the black cat in front of a black wall will be too light. If you want to improve on this, you can set the flash and the camera to manual flash mode or use the flash unit's exposure compensation setting.

Simple TTL Auto Fill Flash: This automatic feature makes a preliminary flash correction automatically but does not sufficiently consider continuous light or background brightness when determining the aperture and shutter speed (compared with matrix-controlled TTL fill flash).

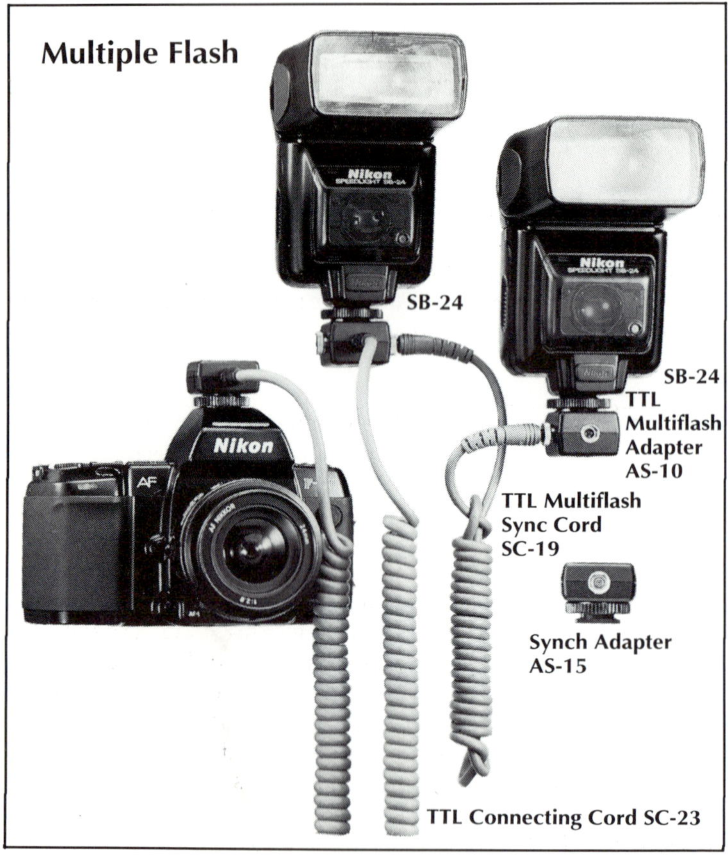

The TTL multiple-flash options shown here with an SB-24 also work with the SB-25.

Matrix Controlled Auto Fill Flash: In this mode, the N6006 and N8008s camera's computer links the automatic continuous light exposure with TTL-controlled flash metering. In practice this means in autoflash mode using matrix metering, the background light and the subject contrast are taken into consideration. With this method, the autoflash preselects the aperture and/or the shutter speed before the flash is fired, and then adjusts the duration of the flash based on the light reflected off the film during exposure. This may be activated in all exposure modes such as aperture priority, shutter priority and programmed autoflash, as well as in manual exposure mode. However, matrix-controlled flash mode is most effective only with automatic programming because in this case the full range of shutter speeds and apertures is accessible automatically.

Overview of Nikon System Flash Units

Nikon manufactures a range of flash units which are suitable for use with Nikon cameras. The table on page 120 is an overview of the features found on these units.

Using Flash with the N6000 Series

The Built-in Flash

To activate the on-board flash (N6006), press the flash lock-release buttons on both sides of the flash. This causes the flash to pop up and automatically turn on. When the flash is ready to fire, a ready-light in the form of a lightning bolt appears in the viewfinder display. This indicator confirms that the capacitor is charged, meaning that the flash is ready to fully discharge.

The built-in flash is capable of performing most of the same functions as supplementary flash units but it has less light output. The two main reasons why people select add-on flashes are to increase light output and to reduce the possibility of "red-eye".

General Flash Data

The operations for all dedicated-flash units, when used on the Nikon N6000 series cameras (totally different from other Nikon

Model No.	Guide Number† feet/meters	Focal length	Batteries	Recycling time (sec.)	No. of flashes (approx.)	Built-in AF-Illuminator	Automatic Fill Flash
SB-16B	105/32	28-85mm manual zoom head	4 AA	11	100	No	Yes
SB-20	100/30	28-85mm zoom head	4 AA	6	160	Yes	Yes
SB-22	83/25	28-35mm diffuser panel	4 AA	4	200	Yes	Yes
SB-23	66/20	35mm	4 AA	2	400	Yes	Yes
SB-24	138/42	24-85mm motorized zoom head	4 AA	7	100	Yes	Yes
SB-25	138/42	24-85mm motorized zoom head, 20mm diffuser panel	4 AA	7	100	Yes	Yes

† **The guide numbers in this overview table relate to ISO 100 and a focal length of 50mm.**

bodies), are approximately the same, but there are some variations. This book will deal with the flashes currently offered for sale by Nikon which are dedicated to the N6000-series cameras. Other after market units may function properly, but it is advised that the photographer consult the flash unit's instruction book before using them with the camera.

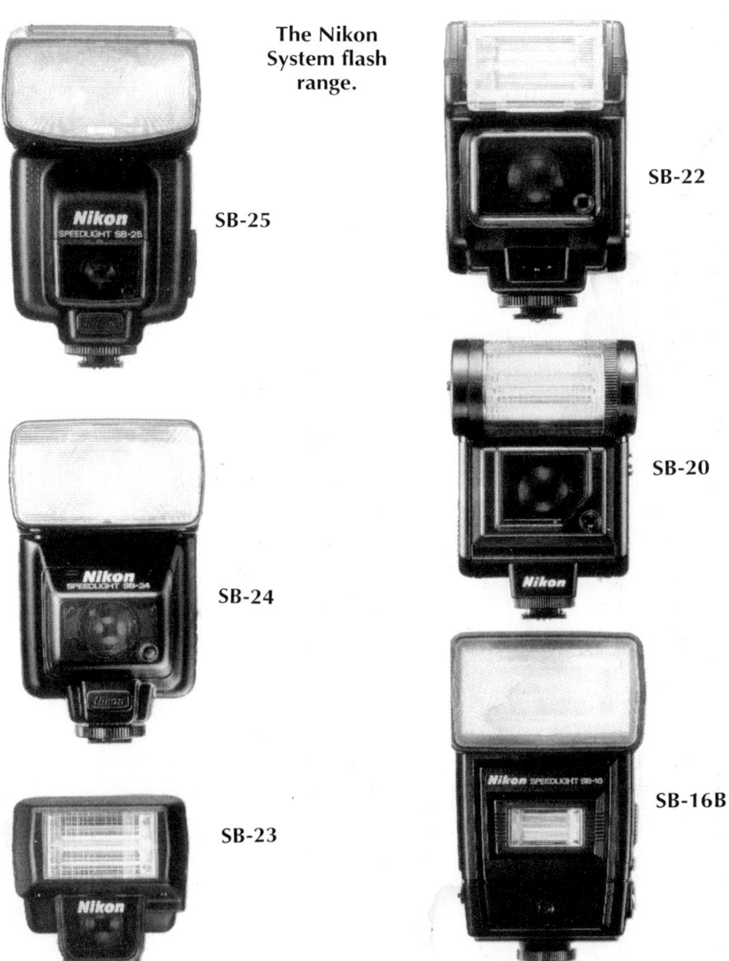

The Nikon System flash range.

SB-25

SB-22

SB-20

SB-24

SB-16B

SB-23

Non-Nikon Flash Units

When non-dedicated flash units are used, the camera should be used in the manual mode. If the flash is in automatic, its automatic system may or may not be employed (at the user's discretion). But a most important fact to remember is that unless a fully dedicated flash is used on the shoe or with a fully dedicated connecting cord (SC-17 TTL Remote Cord, see page 134), TTL flash metering is not possible.

Some after-market flash units claim to be TTL, but may not be fully dedicated for all camera/flash functions. Many contain most of the TTL functions, but not all. When considering the purchase of an after market flash, its instruction book should be consulted before the sale is complete. All of the TTL functions may not be important to some users, but the smart buyer knows what he is getting before money changes hands.

What features are not available from some after-market flashes? The most common is the lack of the flash ready-light symbol in the viewfinder display. But other, more important features may also be missing from these units. The only way to know what is lacking is to know all the features that a Nikon flash offers and compare the differences.

TTL Flash Mode

To use a flash in the TTL mode, turn it on and set it to TTL. Then look into the viewfinder, compose the picture and partially depress the shutter-release button. Check the shutter and lens settings to be sure they are to your liking; make sure the analog display is not warning of underexposure; confirm that the flash-to-subject distance is correct; be sure the ready light is on, then the exposure can be made.

If the analog display indicates "underexposure," or if the ready light blinks, underexposure may occur. Check everything and determine the best course of action. In this mode, the two most practical ways to deliver more light to the film are to open the lens' aperture more or to move closer to the subject.

Camera Exposure Modes with TTL Flash

Program Mode: To use this mode, the camera must be set to either "P" or "Pm" (requires lenses with a built-in CPU). Set the lens to its smallest aperture setting (largest f/number). Turn the

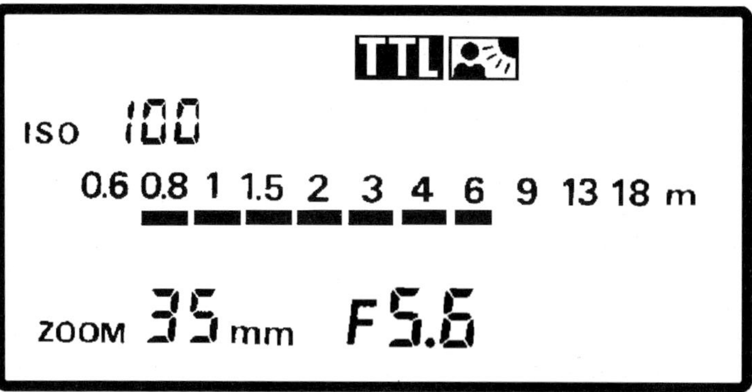

Liquid crystal display (LCD) on the SB-25 flash unit using TTL auto fill-flash. The fill-flash symbol appears whenever automatic fill-flash is used with TTL flash control. This slightly reduces the flash exposure but does not affect the camera's ambient metering system (center-weighted, spot or matrix).

flash unit on and wait for the ready-light. Set the flash unit's mode selector to TTL, if it is not already in that position. If "P", "Pm" or "FEE" blinks, check the above steps because something was omitted. Now press the shutter release button partially down to confirm aperture and shutter speed settings. At this point, the exposure may be taken.

Each ISO/aperture/lens combination will produce a maximum distance capability. The chart on the back of the flash or in the instruction book will list these distances. If the photographer takes pictures that exceed these distances, underexposure might occur.

Shutter Priority Mode:. Set the camera's mode to "S". Remember, only lenses with built-in CPUs can be used in this mode. Again, the lens must be set at its minimum aperture (largest f/stop number). You may now select any shutter speed that is 1/125 of a second or slower. If the shutter speed is set to any speed above 1/125, the camera automatically overrides this choice and sets it to 1/125 when the flash unit is turned on. If a slower shutter speed is selected, a smaller aperture will automatically be selected (depending on ambient light exposure value). This can limit the maximum flash distance.

When all, or most, of the light available for the exposure comes from the flash, the only factor that controls exposure is the aperture. This is because the shutter speed is much slower than the flash duration; thus, the flash duration becomes the effective shutter speed. In situations where we are mixing light, flash plus ambient, the shutter speed is most important. In this case, lens opening and shutter speed are the key factors in determining the total exposure; the flash merely supplements the ambient light.

On rare occasions the flash may, however, be used to overpower the ambient light. These determinations come with experience, and the only way to gain it is through experimentation. Every time a situation arises where you begin to wonder, "what if?" the recommended procedure is: shoot the shot in a safe way, then shoot it again, trying something new. Always record these experiments and soon they will be part of your regular repertoire.

When the lens is set and the shutter speed has been selected, turn the flash unit on. Make sure that the flash is set to the TTL position, look in the viewfinder, compose and confirm the settings. If everything including the flash-to-subject distance is correct, when the ready-light comes on the exposure can be made.

Warnings: If the ready-light (in both the viewfinder and the flash unit) blinks for a few seconds after the exposure, the flash exposure is insufficient for proper exposure. This may or may not indicate underexposure. Check everything carefully if this happens, then decide on the best course of action.

Aperture Priority Mode: First, set the exposure mode to "A", then set the desired aperture on the lens. Now turn the flash unit on and set it to TTL. You may now look in the viewfinder, compose and verify exposure by pressing the shutter release part way. When the ready light comes on, the picture may be taken.

This flash mode has many useful purposes. We have learned the advantages that come to those who know how to control lens settings. The depth-of-field rules apply to flash as well as ambient light photography. But in flash photography, aperture can also effect flash recycle time.

In battery powered electronic flash units, the power from the batteries trickles into a capacitor and the capacitor delivers the power to fire the flash tube. In modern flashes, a thyristor circuit allows unused power to be recycled back into the capacitor. Therefore, if less power is needed there is less drain on the power supply and recycle time is greatly reduced (a benefit of TTL operation as not all the power is used). So we encounter another compromise: what is more important, depth-of-field or rapid flash recycle time? The photographer is in control.

Manual Exposure Mode

In this mode the user has full control of exposure. Naturally, the mode selector must be set to "M". Then set the desired lens aperture and shutter speed. If a shutter speed of 1/250 or faster is selected the camera will automatically reset to 1/125 when the flash unit is turned on. If "bulb" is selected, the camera will revert to TTL, but no exposure information will be displayed.

Many combinations of modes and settings are possible with the N6000-series cameras with the numerous flash units available. The camera may be in the manual mode and the flash in the manual mode, the automatic mode or the TTL mode. We will assume that most flashes will be used in the TTL mode and cover that type of operation.

A shutter speed of 1/250 second is too fast for flash synchronization. Even in Manual mode, when the flash is turned on, the camera will automatically set a shutter speed of 1/125 second.

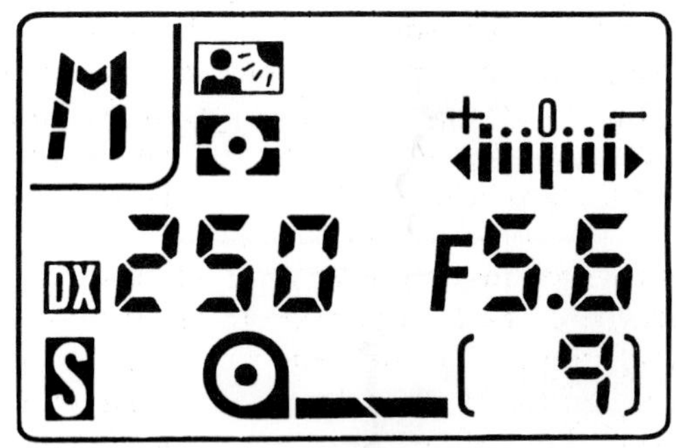

Slow Sync

The slow sync setting is used in program mode for more pleasing ambient light exposure. With normal program mode, the camera automatically selects a flash synchronization speed between 1/60 second and 1/125 second. When the camera is set for SLOW sync the camera will select a shutter speed as low as 30 seconds depending on conditions.

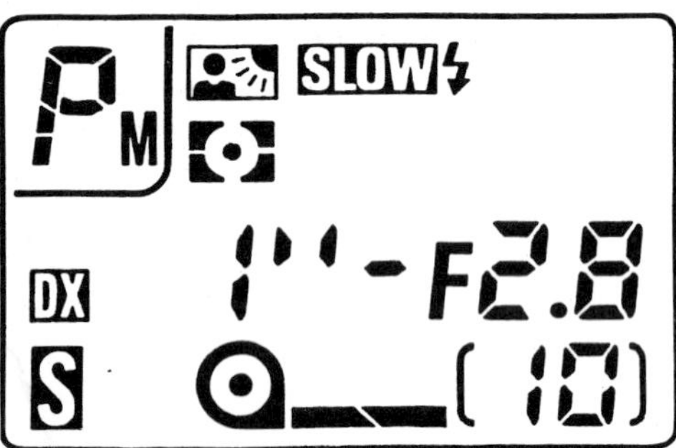

The LCD panel of the N6006 indicating that SLOW flash sync has been selected.

Creating Motion Blurs

When using flash, motion blurs may be created intentionally. The flash image which is sharp due to the brief duration of the flash exposure is superimposed over a second, blurred available light image taken at a slow shutter speed. This can produce very interesting results. The time when the flash is fired during the long exposure determines whether the motion streaks appear in front of the subject or behind it.

Rear Curtain Sync (Second Curtain Sync)

Normally the flash is fired at the beginning of an exposure, but this means the motion streaks lead forward from the sharp image and tend to make it appear as though it were moving backwards.

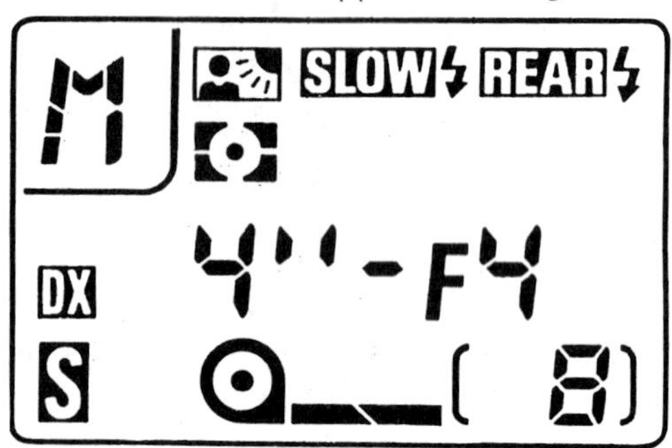

The LCD panel of the N6006 indicating that REAR sync has been selected.

A preferable effect is achieved by firing the flash just before the end of the exposure instead of at the beginning. This is flash synchronization with the second shutter curtain, commonly called "rear curtain sync" Using this technique, the slow ambient light exposure creates motion streaks due to subject movement; then, at the end, the sharp flash exposure is added. This means the motion streaks are placed behind the sharp image of the subject, a much more natural effect that can be "read" more easily by the viewer.

To access this function, press both the SHIFT button and the REAR curtain sync button. Confirm that the REAR sync symbol is displayed before proceeding.

Matrix Balanced Fill Flash

A confusing point in the instruction manual is the term Matrix Balanced Fill Flash. This does not mean the light coming from the flash is being read by a matrix metering pattern. The flash TTL sensor is center-biased, not matrix. What Matrix Balanced Fill Flash means is the ambient light is being read by the matrix meter which determines the correct exposure for the ambient light. This information is based, in part, on what the flash is doing, which is filling in the ambient light.

And no matter if the flash is the fill or key light source, it is being measured by a center-biased TTL meter. The center-weighted section of the viewing screen that is used for this can be imagined by the photographer. The section starts in the lower left corner of the screen. From this point, draw a line up to the small circle, following its curve down until a straight line can be drawn to the lower right corner of the screen. This meter can be fooled just as a center-weighted ambient light meter by light or dark subjects. Unlike an ambient light meter though, we cannot see the light with our eyes to determine if the meter is being fooled. This comes from experience.

Center Weighted Fill Flash

In this mode, the ambient light exposure is measured via center-weighted metering. The flash exposure is measured by the separate center-biased TTL meter. This is not as reliable a system as the matrix balanced fill flash for the majority of situations.

Spot Fill Flash

Same as center-weighted fill flash except ambient light is measured by the spot meter. Only available on N6006.

Using Automatic Balanced Fill Flash

Mount the flash unit on the camera or engage the built-in flash (N6006), making sure first that all the flash's requirements have been met.

The camera's command center should be set at matrix for matrix balanced fill flash, center-weighted position for center-weighted fill flash, or at the spot for spot fill flash. The fill flash symbol will appear when the shift button and the fill flash button are simultaneously pressed. Remember that only AF or AI-P lenses will allow matrix metering. (This is true at any time, when shooting flash or not.)

Automatic balanced fill flash can also be performed in the aperture-priority or manual exposure mode. The same camera setting rules apply. The advantage of using either of these two modes is that the aperture is set by the photographer, thus controlling depth-of-field.

The Nikon N6000 series cameras are capable of performing all the TTL flash-metering functions at any ISO from 25 to 1000. (This is true in any TTL flash mode, fill flash or standard TTL flash photography.)

Using the N8008s with Flash

TTL is an amazing system as it works literally at the speed of light. How does it work? The light from the flash is fired and strikes the subject where it lights it, bounces off, and then reflects back to the camera. This reflected light then passes through the lens, strikes the film plane then bounces down to the sensor in the mirror box. Here the light is read and as the exposure value builds up, the flash is left on. Once the exposure reaches the correct value, the camera's computer turns off the flash. This is a radical departure from traditional flash exposure techniques where the flash blasts off all of its light each time and correct exposure must be manually calculated.

This system relies on new technology called Cybernetic Sync.

A Cyber is an electronic device that performs tasks automatically. In this instance, it's the computer in the N8008s that is the cyber. Nikon's cybernetic control (the special software) automatically adjusts both shutter speed (for ambient light) and aperture (for flash) for correct exposure. This is what makes the system accurate for fill flash.

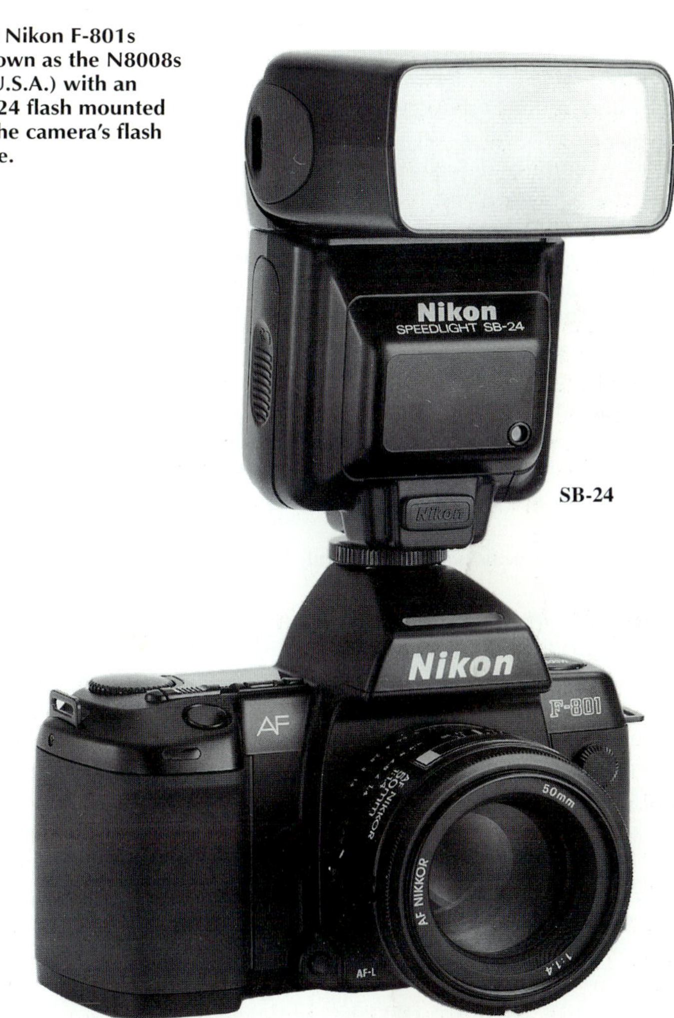

The Nikon F-801s (known as the N8008s in U.S.A.) with an SB-24 flash mounted in the camera's flash shoe.

Any of the three metering modes, Matrix, Center-weighted and Spot can be selected to evaluate background, or ambient light. The aperture selected by the photographer is then taken into consideration for the proper exposure of the background/ambient light as well as the flash. The Cyber balances the exposure of the flash by turning off the flash at the appropriate exposure to balance the ambient light and flash. The flash output, with the flash set to automatic TTL, will be in the range of 1:1 lighting to a minus 1 2/3 stops. But the computer tends to settle with a minus 2/3 stop minus compensation for the flash exposure whenever possible. (The use of automatic and standard TTL with the N8008s is fully described in the *Magic Lantern Guide to Nikon SB-25*.)

Operating the N8008s with the SB-25 Flash

Following is a brief introduction to the steps in basic operation of the N8008s with the SB-24 and SB-25, including brief references to common problem areas, sources of misunderstandings.

Film speed: The ISO film speed is transferred automatically to the SB-24 or SB-25 when the N8008s camera is used. To manually set the film speed, use the following procedure.

1. Use the SEL button to select the film speed field on the LCD.
2. It blinks.
3. The value may now be set with the arrow keys.

Mounting the unit on the camera: Be sure that the flash foot is seated properly in the camera's flash shoe, then tighten the locking screw.

Selecting the flash operating mode: Use the sliding switch to select the main operating mode between TTL autoflash - "TTL," stroboscopic - "multi-flash symbol," manual flash - "M," and non-TTL automatic flash - "A." The selected flash mode is indicated on the flash unit's LCD panel.

Selecting the synchronization: For general photography, the sliding switch should be set on "NORMAL." "REAR" should be used only in conjunction with slow synchronization if second shutter curtain sync is desired (see page 134).

Adjusting the zoom head: When AF and AI-P Nikkor lenses are used with a N8008/s camera the flash unit's zoom head is adjusted automatically. With NON-AF Nikkor lenses, the zoom head must be adjusted manually by pushing the zoom button. The SB-25's 20mm diffuser panel must be pulled out and down manually.

Flash head position: The normal locked position is facing forward. To adjust the flash head position, the lateral lock lever must be released. If the -7° tilt feature is in use, the range indicator blinks to remind the user that the flash head is not in the normal position. In any other "non-normal" position such as bounce, the distance scale is blank since the flash cannot gauge the potential range would be.

Determining the distance for a preset aperture: When using the flash modes "M" and "TTL" in conjunction with the N8008 camera and AF and AI-P Nikkor lenses, the selected aperture value is automatically transferred to the SB-25. With NON-AF Nikkor lenses the f/stop must first be set on the lens and then again, manually on the SB-24 or SB-25 for correct exposure range information.

1. Press the SEL button.
2. Aperture position on the LCD blinks.
3. Adjust with the arrow switches.

The LCD display indicates the correct distance setting (manual flash) or the flash range (TTL flash) in the form of bars on the range scale.

Determining the aperture for a pre-determined distance: To accomplish this, N8008s camera used in conjunction with AF and AI-P Nikkor lenses, require that the aperture be adjusted on the camera lens until the LCD on the SB-24 or SB-25 indicates the desired distance or distance range. With the use of NON-AF Nikkor lenses, the aperture must be adjusted on the SB-24 or SB-25 until the desired distance setting is indicated on the LCD display; this aperture value is then also set on the lens.

Changing the output level: In "M" mode the M button may be pressed for a continuous selection of flash output from 1/1 (full) to 1/64.

Flash exposure compensation: To may make flash exposure adjustments in TTL mode on the SB-24 and SB-25. The SEL button is used to activate the correction field on the LCD and then the arrow keys are used to select the desired correction value.

Program Modes with Flash

In program modes, the shutter sync speed of 1/250 takes priority over all other sync speeds. When the aperture is closed down and reaches its limit, the computer will hold the shutter speed to 1/60 (if flash is set to "normal", otherwise it will go down to 30 seconds). The 1/60 speed is selected to prevent subject blur which can be caused by movement during the ambient light exposure. The aperture range in these modes is f/4 to the lens' smallest f/stop.

Shutter Priority (S): In this mode, the photographer can select any shutter speed from 30 seconds to 1/250 no matter what mode the flash is set to. The aperture is set by the computer within the limits of its range. The "HI" symbol can still appear when using flash indicating that the ambient light, and not the flash, will be over exposed. The analog scale will appear if the aperture and shutter speed combo will underexpose the ambient light. This does not indicate the flash is underexposing.

Manual Mode (M): In manual, the photographer selects both the shutter speed and aperture. The TTL system will still take care of the flash exposure and will balance it with the ambient light exposure. Even if the photographer improperly exposes for the ambient light, the camera will properly expose the subject though the entire scene could be dark or light. In the "S" and "M" modes, if the photographer selects a shutter speed of 1/500 or higher, the camera will automatically set the shutter speed to 1/250. This prevents taking flash photographs out of sync.

Matrix Balanced Fill Flash

A confusing point in the instruction manual is the term Matrix Balanced Fill Flash. This does not mean the light coming from the flash is being read by a matrix metering pattern. The flash TTL sensor is center-biased, not matrix. What Matrix Balanced Fill Flash means is the ambient light is being read by the matrix meter which determines the correct exposure for the ambient light. This information is based, in part, on what the flash is doing, which is filling in the ambient light.

And no matter if the flash is the fill or key light source, it is being measured by a center-biased TTL meter. The center-weighted section of the viewing screen that is used for this can be imagined by the photographer. The section starts in the lower left corner of the screen. From this point, draw a line up to the small circle, following its curve down until a straight line can be drawn to the lower right corner of the screen. This meter can be fooled just as a center-weighted ambient light meter by light or dark subjects. Unlike a ambient light meter though, we cannot see with our eyes the light to determine if the meter is being fooled. This comes from experience.

Using Matrix Balanced Fill Flash: The N8008s, with AF or AI-P Nikkor lenses, works with the SB-24 and SB-25 in matrix metering mode when set on program, shutter or aperture priority with matrix-balanced TTL fill flash. Manual camera exposure mode may be used but the background or ambient light must be adjusted manually in a very specific manner. The N8008s camera may also be switched to center-weighted or spot TTL fill-in auto-flash mode. The following is the step-by-step procedure for Matrix Balanced Fill Flash:

1. Mount the SB-24 or SB-25 in the camera accessory shoe and switch on camera and flash.
2. Set the flash on "TTL" mode.
3. The flash unit's LCD will display the TTL symbol and the matrix symbol.
4. The film speed and the zoom reflector (with AF or AI-P lenses) are adjusted automatically.
5. Aperture values are transferred to the flash.
6. Select an automatic exposure mode or manual exposure setting. With manual exposure or shutter priority a flash synchronization speed up to 1/250 sec. can be selected.
7. Focus on your subject.
8. Check whether the distance range displayed by the LCD is appropriate for the distance to the subject. If necessary, adjust the aperture setting on the lens until it is appropriate for the indicated distance range.
9. Now, press the shutter release.

Manual Flash Operation

The following is the basic procedure for manually setting the SB-24 or SB-25 with an N8008s camera:

1. Mount the flash to the camera accessory shoe and switch on the camera and flash.
2. Select "M" mode on the flash unit.
3. Set your camera on manual exposure or aperture priority. In manual flash mode the LCD panel will "receive" the aperture settings from the camera automatically.
4. Focus on your subject.
5. Adjust the aperture on the lens and on the flash unit until the distance indicated on the flash unit's LCD corresponds to the subject distance.
6. Press the shutter release.

Limitations of Manual Flash: When using just a guide number calculation, perfect flash exposures are rare. This is because ambient light and subject characteristics play an important role in the overall exposure. Manual flash exposures using a flash exposure meter are more reliable. It is best to make a series of bracketed exposures, in fixed increments over and under the calculated exposure when using manual flash.

Rear Curtain Sync (Second Curtain Sync)

With normal synchronization (with the first shutter curtain) the moving subject will "push" its motion blur in front of the sharp image. This occurs because the sharp flash exposure occurred at the beginning of the movement. With rear or second curtain sync, the flash fires just before the shutter closes causing the sharp subject to "drag" its motion blur. This corresponds with the natural way we perceive motion. Rear Curtain Sync "REAR" must be selected on the SB-24 or SB-25 Flash when using it with the N8008s camera.

Nikon Accessory Cords and Adapters

SC-17 TTL Remote Cord

One end of this 4.9′ (1.5 m) coiled cable has a flash connector which slides into the shoe of the N6000/N6006 and N8008s

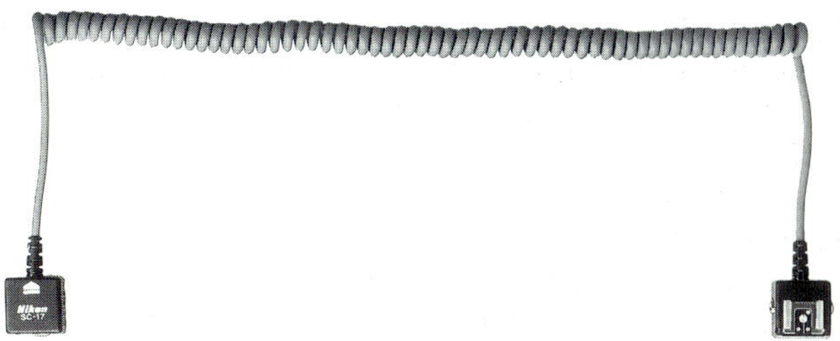

TTL Remote Cord SC-17

cameras. It relays information between the camera and flash. The other side of the cable has a flash shoe and two multi-flash sockets for attaching any Nikon systems flash unit or the connection of additional flash units via additional TTL cables (SC-18 or SC-19). With N6000/N6006 and N8008s cameras, the SC-17 allows all TTL flash functions with all camera-specific options The SC-17 is necessary for using the flash off-camera or in conjunction with a flash bracket such as "Stroboframe".

Multiflash Sync Cords

TTL extension cables SC-18 and SC-19 are also called "TTL-Multiflash-Cords." These feature connectors on both sides for Nikon multiflash system components (such as the SC-17 Cord,

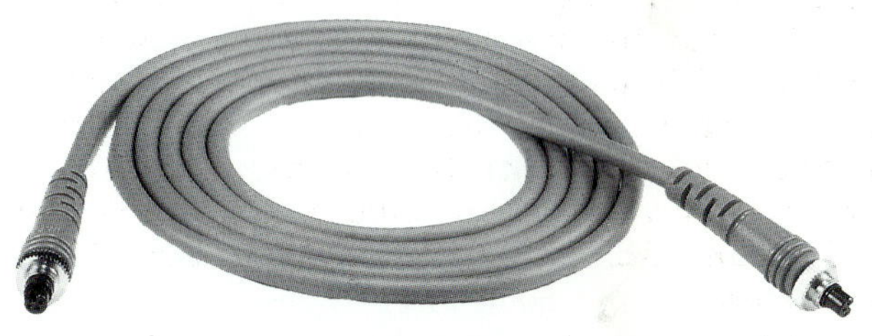

TTL Multiflash Sync Cord SC-18

Multiflash Adapter AS-10, and Nikon systems flash units). They transmit all Nikon systems commands with all camera-specific options.

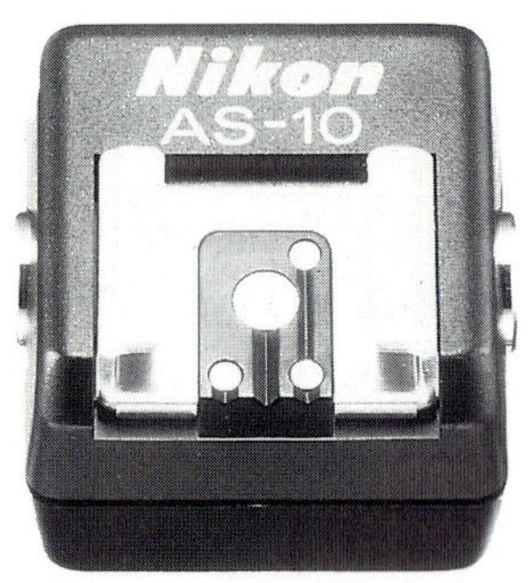

TTL-Multiflash Adapter AS-10.

TTL-Multiflash Adapter AS-10

TTL-Multiflash Adapter AS-10
For multiple flash with more than three flash units. One flash mounts directly on the AS-10's shoe, the rest are connected to its multiflash sockets using the SC-18 or SC-19 cord.

Non-Nikon Flash Units

For other flash units, the flash's instruction book will give you some basic data, but possibly not all the information you need. Since there are countless electronic flash units and cameras on the market, their instruction books may not cover their use on every camera.

Additional Information

Many fine books with detailed flash information are available at your local camera store. Some that may answer Nikon flash questions are: *Magic Lantern Guide to Nikon SB-25 Flash System, The Advanced Nikon System* from Magic Lantern Guides, *Nikon Compendium* from Hove Books®, and *Magic Lantern Guide to Metz Flash Systems.* These are available from your dealer, or write for a complete catalog from Silver Pixel Press, Division of The Saunders Group, 21 Jet Drive, Rochester, NY 14624.

Nikkor Lenses

An Overview of Nikon Lens Technology

A lens can be evaluated by many standards, not the least of which is, "will the lens do the right job for the right price?" While this is a subjective determination, a lens can be judged objectively by standards of resolution, distortion, light falloff, sharpness, chromatic aberration, mechanical durability and focusing speed. The following is a brief overview of some of the characteristics that make Nikkor lenses the top choice of many photographers.

The Metal Bayonet Mount

The bayonet mount on Nikon cameras and lenses is made from high-performance metal alloys designed to function well in a wide range of conditions from arctic to tropical. A perfectly parallel film plane and lens plane is critical for sharp results as is the distance from the film plane to the bayonet mount. This so-called mounting specification must be accurate to 1/100 mm. Consequently, if a lens' bayonet mount is damaged (usually due to impact on the front while mounted on the camera), send it to Nikon service immediately. The distance will be measured from all four corners of the film plane and the bayonet will be justified or replaced. Generally, it is not possible to perform this kind of work on plastic bayonets, which is one of the reasons Nikon has kept its time-proven metal bayonet mount.

Optimization for Close-up and Long Range

Before computer-aided lens design and modern technological innovations, it was not possible to optimize lenses so that they performed equally well at both close and long range. Lenses were either optimized for infinity or for the close-up range. With the addition of movable optical elements, typical close-up defects, such as barrel distortion or aberration, can now be corrected. By using this close-range correction (CRC), Nikon has manufactured lenses which are equally suitable for normal-range and close-up photography. This technology has also been incorporated in the construction of modern Nikon zoom lenses.

Chromatic Aberration and ED Lenses

Chromatic aberration can be a problem in lenses with long focal lengths. This is caused by the fact that blue, green and red light do not focus at a common point. This failure causes colored outlines that effect sharpness. A true apochromatic lens eliminates this phenomenon. These lenses are constructed using glass with extremely low dispersion characteristics, called LD or ED glass (Low or Extraordinary Dispersion). This allows the three colors to focus as close to the same point as possible, thus, there is virtually no separation of the light into its spectral components. This results in virtually no chromatic aberration. All modern Nikkors and AF-Nikkors with a focal length of 180mm or above contain elements of ED glass for apochromatic correction.

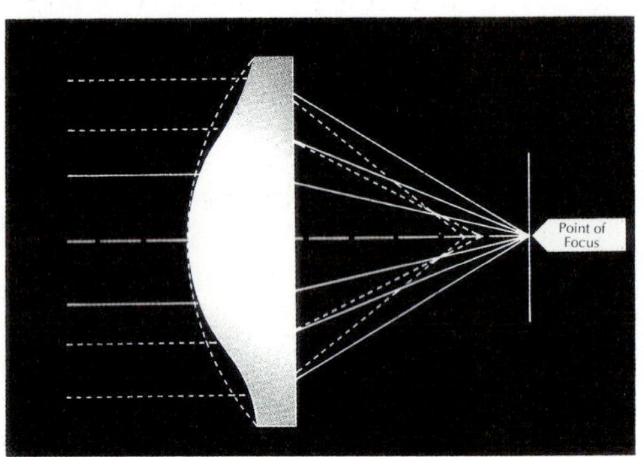

Aspherical lens elements have a non-spherical curvature which allows them to focus light rays striking all parts of the lens surface at a common plane.

Spherical Aberration and Aspherical Elements

Spherical aberration occurs in optical elements with spherically-curved surfaces because the light passing through the edge of an element does not converge at exactly the same point as the light passing through its center. The resulting loss of sharpness is called spherical aberration. Today, the use of aspherical elements allows lenses to be constructed which correct for this problem. This ensures sharpness and brilliance even with high speed lenses.

Internal Focusing

Before internal focusing was incorporated into telephoto lenses, the actual length of the lens changed during focusing. This made manual focusing very awkward and inexact. With IF lenses, the total length of the lens remains constant. Focusing is achieved by shifting the position of an optical element group inside the lens between the main element groups. This element group actually only needs to move a short distance. Internal focus lenses not only allow faster, more precise manual focusing, but also provide unbeatable speed in automatic focusing. In addition, internal focusing can be combined with automatic correction, which leads to a general improvement in the quality of reproduction.

Variable f/stop Design

A variable f/stop zoom lens changes its effective f/stop as it is zoomed (refer to the tech sheet that accompanies the lens for exact specifics). This allows smaller, more compact lenses to be designed, such as the 35-70mm which many photographers find a pleasure to use. Some photographers find the change in effective f/stop somewhat confusing, however, those who take advantage of the camera's program modes need not be concerned with this.

Brief History of Nikon Lenses

Non-AI Nikkors

When this generation of lenses appeared, complex automatic exposure functions didn't exist; the catch phrase of the day was "open-aperture metering." This replaced the cumbersome stopped-down metering function found on early 35mm SLRs. With open-aperture metering, the aperture ring is set to a metering value but the aperture remains wide open for viewing. In order to allow accurate exposure metering, the selected aperture must be transmitted to the camera's exposure meter.

In the case of non-AI Nikkor lenses, this connection occurs by means of a fork. When the lens was fitted, a cam located above the camera's bayonet mount engaged with this fork. As the aperture ring was turned, the cam automatically moved with it, thus transmitting the setting of the aperture ring to the camera. In order to meter the exposure, the camera had to know which absolute aperture value corresponded to the relative position of the aperture ring, the lens had to be adjusted to its "maximum aperture setting" (lens speed) after being fitted. This is why Nikon photographers always turned the aperture ring after changing a lens. The aperture fork made the metering procedure itself faster and simpler, but changing lenses was a little awkward.

AI Lenses
Aperture Indexing lenses made lens changes even more simple. The lenses communicated the aperture through a mechanical coding, and the camera bayonet mount featured a mechanical cam for reading this data. In addition, the aperture fork was replaced by a cam integrated in the lens mount into which the reading pin of the camera's cam automatically clicked when the lens was twisted into place.

Note: *AI lenses can generally be used on modern AF cameras such as the N6000, N6006 and N8008s, with manual focus and restricted exposure metering and automatic exposure functions. Various AI-Nikkors of older production runs, certain extension tubes and some non-AF special-purpose lenses like some fish-eyes or older PC-Nikkors may* <u>*not*</u> *be used with modern Nikon cameras. Mechanical or electro-mechanical failure could result!*

AI-S Lenses
When using program mode or shutter priority mode, the lens aperture must be closed down with great precision to the working value calculated by the camera when the shutter is released. This required a completely new transmission mechanism, which was incorporated into the AI-S lenses. AI-S lenses also featured mechanical coding to transmit focal length to the camera.

AI-P Lenses
These lenses feature a built-in microchip or CPU which transmits typical lens data such as minimum and maximum f/stop, set aperture, and focal length to the camera by electronic means. They are, therefore, fully compatible with N6000/N6006 and N8008s cameras except for the AF function.

AF Nikkors Lenses
These lenses not only possess the mechanical coupling for the motorized focusing of the lens, they also contain a built-in microcomputer chip which determines all the lens data required for focusing and exposure. Thus, information on focusing movements, current position of elements, lens speed, aperture setting, and focal length is transmitted to the camera by electronic means.

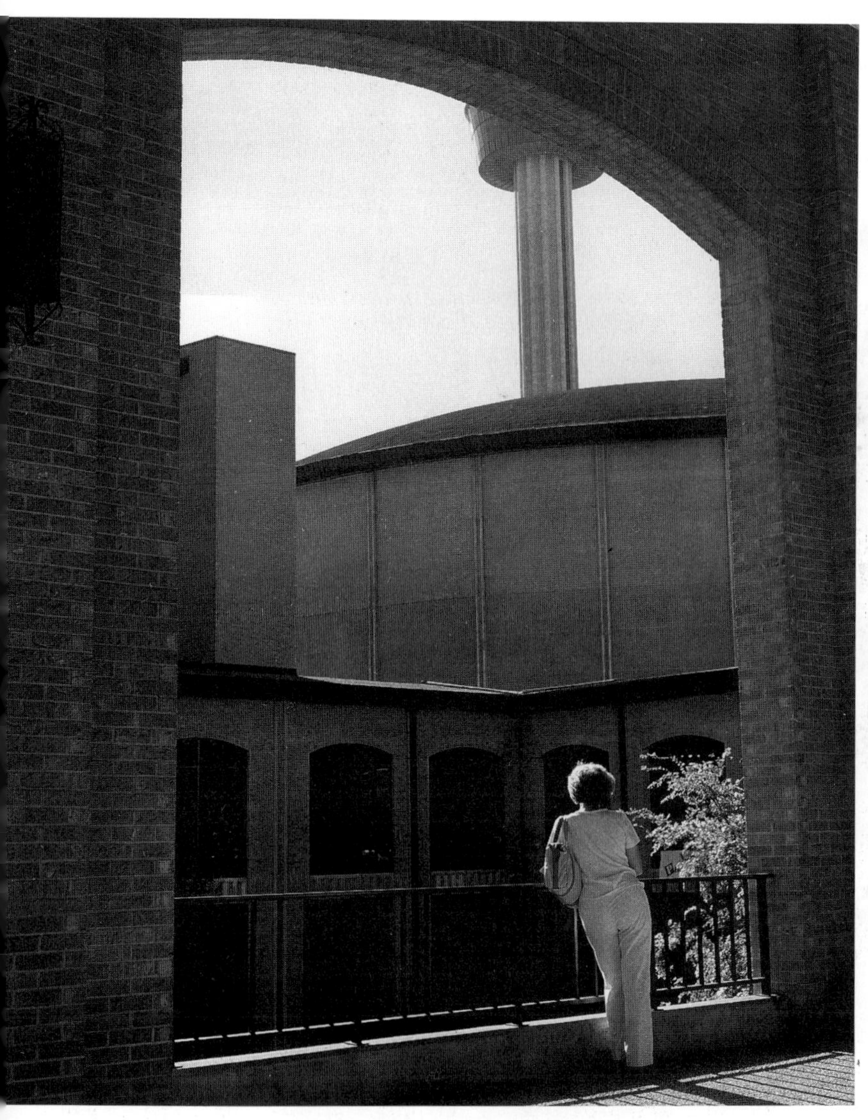

Precise framing is easy when using a versatile lens like the Nikkor 28-85 AF. This picture of the San Antonio Convention Center was taken with the lens set at approximately 80mm.

Nikon AF Lenses

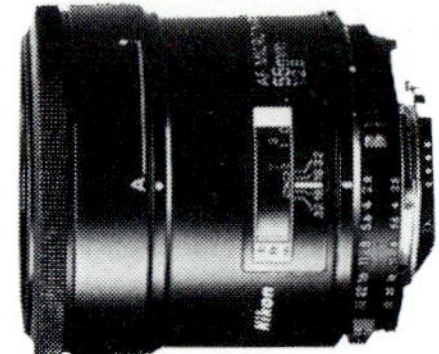

AF-Micro Nikkor
55mm f/2.8

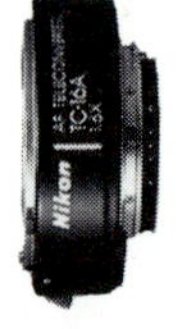

Autofocus
Teleconverter
TC-16A

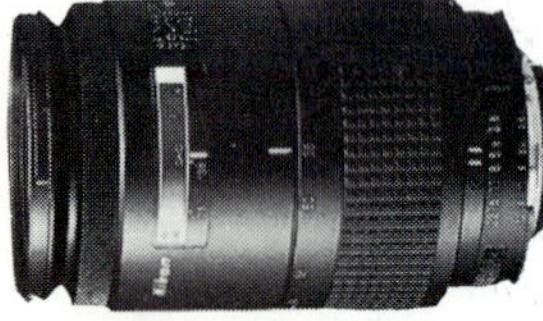

AF Zoom Nikkor
35-135mm f/3.5-4.5

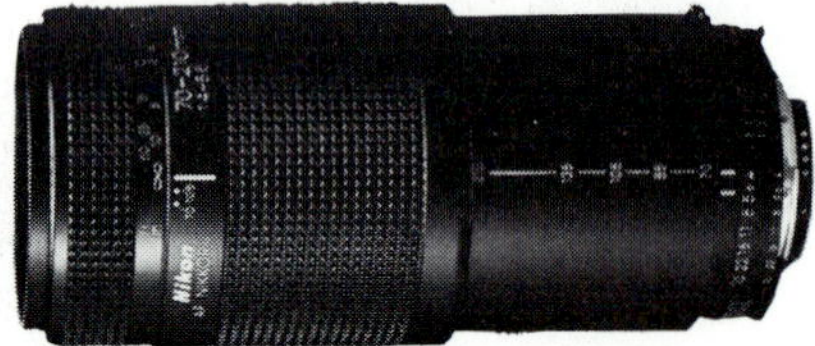

AF Zoom Nikkor
70-210mm f/4-5.6 D

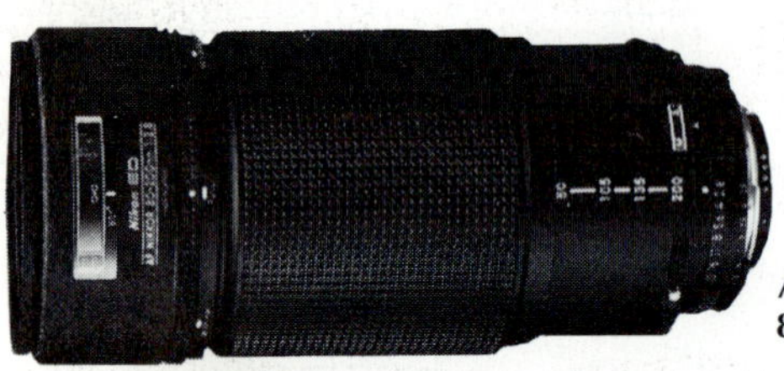

AF Zoom Nikkor
80-200mm f/2.8 ED

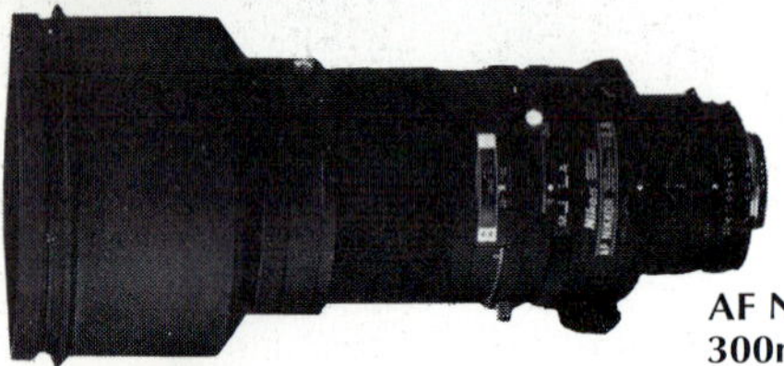

AF Nikkor
300mm f/2.8 IF-ED

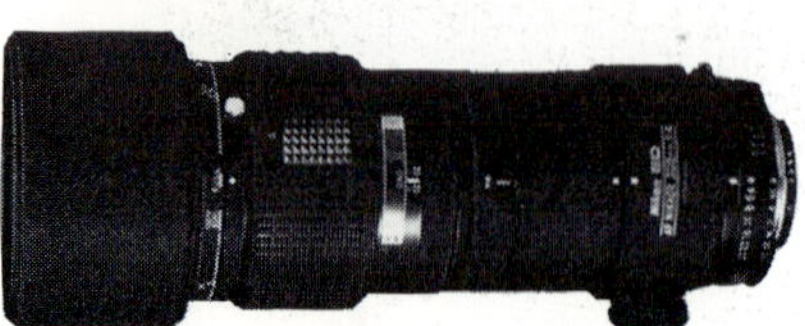

AF Nikkor
300mm f/4 IF-ED

Nikon AF Lenses

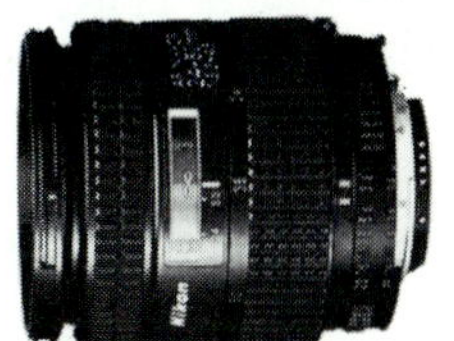

AF Zoom Nikkor
24-50mm f/3.3-4.5

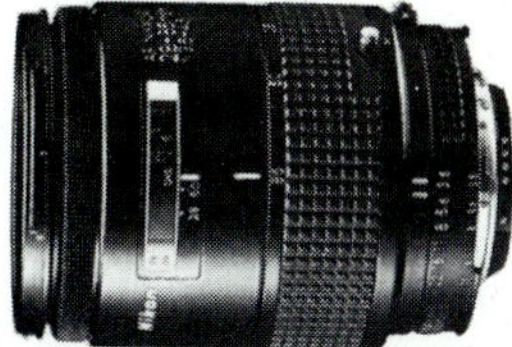

AF Zoom Nikkor
28-85mm f/3.5-4.5

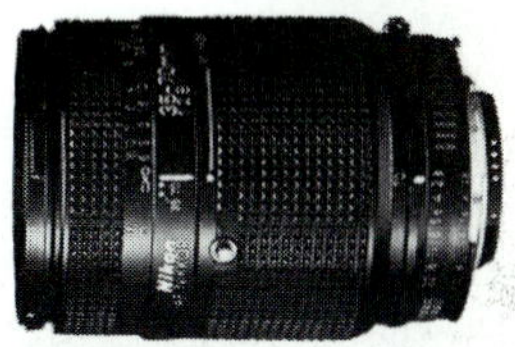

AF Zoom Nikkor
35-70mm f/2.8

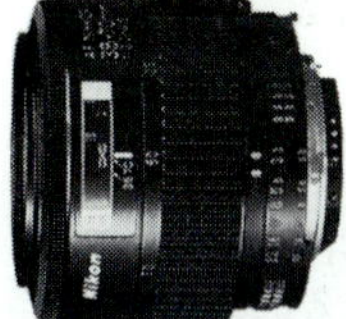

AF Zoom Nikkor
35-70mm f/3.3-4.5

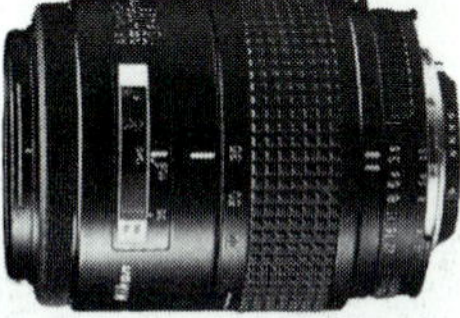

AF Zoom Nikkor
35-105mm f/3.5-4.5

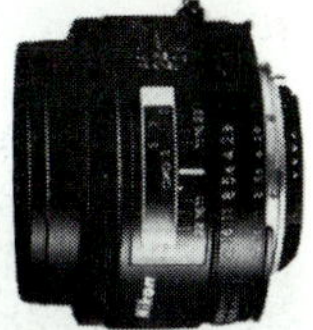

AF Nikkor
24mm f/2.8

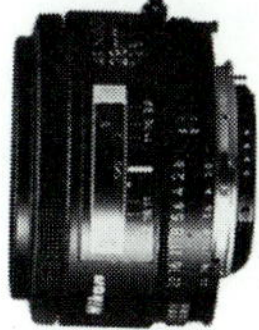

AF Nikkor
28mm f/2.8

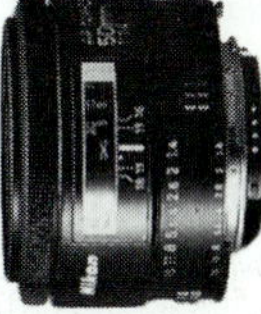

AF Nikkor
50mm f/1.4

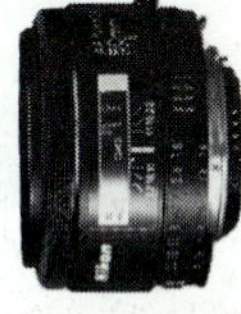

AF Nikkor
50mm f/1.8

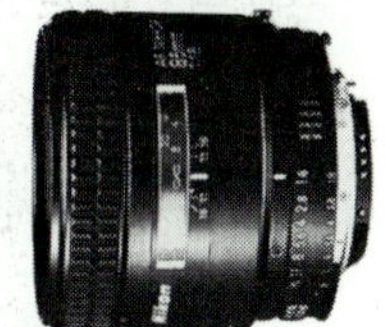

AF Nikkor
85mm f/1.8

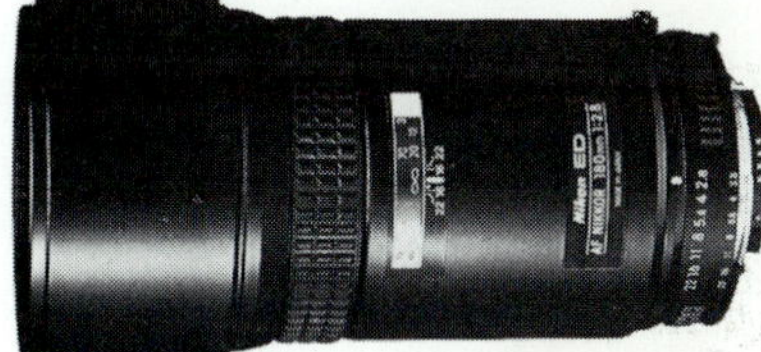

AF Nikkor
180mm f/2.8 IF-ED

AF-D Nikkor Lenses

Previous AF-Nikkors did not give the camera a value for the subject's distance, but rather, simply transmitted a value for the number of motor-revolutions necessary to achieve focus. The chip in the Type D lenses, on the other hand, gives the absolute distance in meters. The 3D "intelligent" exposure and flash modes that are found in the N90/F90 are thus made possible. ***Note:*** The transmission of subject distance can only be used with the N90/F90 and N50/F50 to date. Otherwise, D lenses are fully compatible with all functions in the N6006 and N8008s such as auto exposure.

AF-I Nikkor Lenses with AF Motor

Except for the lack of the AF motor coupling, the bayonet is the same as that on normal AF Nikkors. The AF contacts are the same, but are more extensively utilized. The special feature of the AF-I Nikkors (e.g. the AF- I 300mm f/2.8 D IF-ED) is a super-fast, coreless DC motor which is built into the lens. Focusing distances can be indexed and recalled at any time using the focus lock button. The AF-I lens can also be focused by hand, with the traditional "mechanical" feel. The special feature here is that the lens does not first have to be switched from autofocus to manual, it does so automatically when the focusing ring on the lens is turned. Since all these AF functions require a special interaction with the camera, the AF functions of AF-I lenses can currently only be used in combination with the F4-series cameras and the N90/F90, N50/F50. With the N6000, N6006 and N8008s cameras, these lenses allow all automatic exposure functions but only manual focus.

Lens/Camera Compatibility

There are many lenses that fit the Nikon N-series cameras such as the N6006, N6000, and the N8008s. Nikon manufactures a vast array as do many after-market lens manufacturers. Hundreds of earlier-produced lenses will also function in a satisfactory manner. However, some lenses should not be used on any N-series camera.

VERY IMPORTANT: The following chart is an overview of recommended lens compatibility with N6000/N6006 and N8008s cameras. However, we also suggest that you always read the instruction manuals of both lens and camera before trying to combine units from different generations. If there is still any doubt, consult a knowledgeable Nikon dealer or call Nikon Technical Service.

Nikon Camera and Lens Compatibility*

Lens Type	N6006/N6000	N8008/N8008s
AF Nikkor	+	+
AF-D Nikkor	+	+
AF-I Nikkor	X	X
AI-P Nikkor	+	+
AI-S Nikkor	F	F
AI Nikkor	F	F
AI Converted Nikkor	F	F
Non-AI Nikkor	-	-
Series E Nikkor	F	F
Medical Nikkor	B	B
Reflex and PC Nikkor	A	A
PB-6 Bellows	A	A
Extension Tubes** - PK-11A,		
PK-12, PK-13, PN-11	F	F
TC-14A/B, TC-201/301	A	F
TC-16A	-	F
TC-14E, TC-20E***	X	X

* Possibility of Damage! Certain non-AI Nikkors as well as some older AI Nikkors, extension tubes and several non-AI special purpose lenses such as Fisheyes or older PC Nikkors cannot be used with modern Nikon cameras. Mechanical or electrical damage can result! *This table provides only an overview. Always refer to the camera and lens instruction manual to determine compatibility.

** On AF cameras or with AF Nikkors, only PK-11A may be used, not PK-11 (only BR-2A reversing ring may be used, not BR-2).

*** Data applies only for combinations with AF-I lenses.

\+ Can be used without restrictions.

\- Not compatible. Not recommended or possibility of damage!

X Manual focus only. Auto exposure modes can be used.

A Only with Aperture Priority mode and center-weighted metering. Display readouts may not correspond to actual values.

B Correct exposure only possible with flash.

F Manual exposure or Aperture Priority mode only with center-weighted or spot metering only.

A Tour of Nikkor Lenses

Nikon is well-known as the manufacturer of some of the finest quality optics available today. The line-up of Nikon lenses changes constantly. New lenses are introduced, while old ones are up-graded or discontinued on an ongoing basis. The *Magic Lantern Guide to Nikon Lenses* by B. "Moose" Peterson not only lists most current Nikon lenses, but it also gives the reader a feel for using each individual lens and is a helpful tool in understanding and selecting them. It also recommends several "oldies but goodies" which might be worthwhile to purchase from your dealer's "used case." If you are interested in reading about Nikon lenses in depth, I highly recommend this book. This section is a brief explanation of various types of lenses plus a few suggestions of some popular choices.

Lens Characteristics

Lenses are characterized by two parameters: maximum aperture (or lens speed) and focal length. Maximum aperture indicates the largest opening available on the lens. The aperture opening controls the amount of light that passes through the lens. In effect, a lens aperture works similar to the eye's iris. Aperture openings are expressed as f/stops which are actually fractions. For example, f/16 is a smaller aperture opening than f/11. Therefore f/2.8 is a relatively large aperture. An aperture of f/2 is even larger yet. By opening the lens one full f/stop, twice the amount of light passes to the film. The amount of light is cut in half whenever the aperture is closed down to the next higher f/stop number (i.e. from f/11 to f/16).

The second lens parameter, always indicated in millimeters, these days, expresses focal length. This is usually considered the most important lens reference value and it is independent of any film format. Inside each lens assembly light rays coming from infinity are bent so that they meet in a point of focus. The distance from the rear-nodal point (optical center of the lens) to the film plane is defined as focal length. The image angle covered by a lens is a function of focal length. A larger image angle becomes a wide angle, a small image angle becomes a telephoto, and a variable image angle is characteristic of a zoom lens.

Fisheye Lenses

The days when an image taken with a fisheye lens brought gasps of astonishment to an audience are long gone. Everyone has seen the fisheye effect, maybe even a bit too much. This is not to say that we should renounce the use of fisheye lenses, just that we should use them judiciously. Fisheye lenses are examples of barrel distortion gone wild, and totally uncorrected. The only straight lines which will be rendered straight are those passing through the exact center of the image. Circular and full-frame fisheyes can be used to produce very exaggerated perspectives in views of interiors, or the sweeping panoramas of landscapes in which the distortion will not be obvious unless the lens is tilted up or down. Try using a fisheye for close-ups of flowers, getting all the way down on the ground and looking up at the flower from below. Don't be afraid to try unusual things like this, the photos may be spectacular and certainly will get you to thinking about ways to use these lenses' unusual perspective.

Nikon makes 6mm and 8mm circular fisheyes. These project a completely circular image on a single frame of 35mm film. The price of Nikon's 6mm fisheye is out of range for most photographers although they can be rented. The 8mm, can be easily handheld and is more affordably priced. The 16mm which is a full-frame fisheye with a more realistic price has always been popular and resides in many camera bags for those special times when only a fisheye will do the job.

Ultra Wide-Angle Lenses

Photos taken with ultra wide-angle lenses can be remarkably striking. These lenses lend themselves to providing unusual perspectives and opening up spaces indoors as well as outdoors. One of the most important advantages of ultra wide-angle lenses is that with them, you can take in large areas from very short distances. This is particularly an advantage indoors in cramped surroundings because these lenses can make an area appear more spacious. Advertising photos of auto interiors are generally taken with ultra wide angle lenses for this reason. When viewed through a 20mm, the interior of a car looks open and spacious! These lenses are not just for indoors, they are also very useful around town where quite often it is impossible to stand back far enough to take in a view. They are able to include the balance of a city block from a vantage point across a street.

One prime choice in the ultra wide category is the 20mm f/2.8 AF. It has captured many photographers' attention due to its compact size and reasonable price. It is also a great choice for nature photographers since it combines all of the benefits of the 13mm, 15mm and 18mm with the added advantage of more filtration options.

Wide-Angle Lenses

There is really no clear point when a lens stops being an ultra wide-angle lens and becomes just an ordinary wide-angle. For example, not too long ago a 28mm was considered an exotic ultra wide-angle for many of us. Now the 28mm is a very pedestrian focal length, not regarded as ultra-anything. By today's standards, anything wider than about 24mm is an ultra wide-angle, so we will leave it at that in this book.

The more conservative wide-angle lenses such as 24mm, 28mm and 35mm are much easier to use than the ultra wides because alignment is far less critical. The 24mm can do practically anything that the 20mm can do, you just have to move back a bit more. They are excellent landscape lenses. The perspective is still exaggerated in these lenses, so care must be exercised to keep the camera level. This avoids tipping over buildings and the like.

With the 28mm and 35mm you can easily take more normal-looking photos. You can even use them for portraiture so long as you do not move in too close to your subject. This will distort the subject's features in an unattractive manner.

For certain types of photography wide angle lenses are becoming the norm. One major photojournalist that I know is famous for his environmental portraits for magazines. He nearly always shoots with a 35mm lens. Many fashion photographers take advantage of the perspective of the 28mm or 35mm to photograph models from low angles. This makes their already long slender legs appear to be endless. These lenses are also excellent for group portraits when four or more people must be included in a single image.

The Nikkor 24mm f/2.8 AF is an extremely popular wide angle. This is due to its small size and affordable price tag. It is great for scenic shots. Since it is only twice as wide as normal vision, its wide coverage is "comfortable" and not beyond the realm or imagination of most amateur photographers. It does not have the "distortion" many photographers associate with wide angles.

Normal Lenses

The rule of thumb is that a "normal" lens has a focal length about the same as the diagonal of the film frame. By this rule the normal lens for a 35mm camera should be the diagonal of the frame. In actual practice, most photographers prefer a lens a little bit longer than the precise measure of the diagonal, so the standardized normal lens for 35mm has become something in the 50mm range.

If you were to select a single "normal" AF Nikkor, the 50mm f/1.4 would probably be a first choice. It offers outstanding optical quality together with fast speed. For macro fans, the AF Micro-Nikkor 60mm f/2.8 is an excellent, albeit expensive, choice. This lens offers a reproduction ratio of 1:1 meaning the subject will be lifesize on the film.

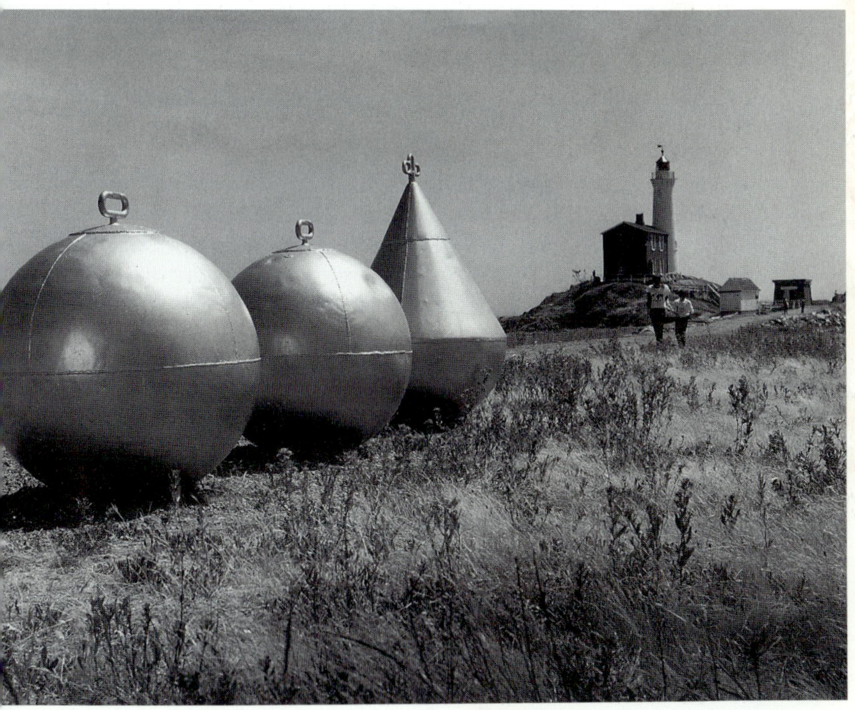

Here is an interesting photo that was shot with a normal lens! Do not underestimate the capabilities of this very versatile lens range.

Short Telephoto Lenses

Short telephoto lenses in the range from 70mm up to about 135mm, are often called portrait lenses, however, they are useful for a large number of subjects other than just for portraits. Because short telephotos are such a popular choice, there are many lenses to choose from in this range.

Lenses in this focal length range are well suited to portraits because they provide an undistorted and flattering perspective for the head-and-shoulders shot. Typically, lenses are used for portraiture at wide apertures to throw backgrounds and foregrounds out of focus and place the emphasis on the subject.

However you should never let the nomenclature of short telephotos as "portrait lenses" persuade you not to use other lenses for portraits. I have often taken portrait photos with lenses in the 180-200mm range. The point is that there are really no rules on which lens to use, only general guidelines. If a particular lens works for you for a particular picture, then it is the correct lens. What really matters behind all of this technical information about cameras and lenses is the final image, ultimately that is all that the viewer sees or cares about.

In this category, the AF 85mm f/1.8 is a relatively economical AF fixed focal length Nikon lens that leaves nothing to be desired. Thanks to its fast speed, this lens allows shots where the subject is in focus and in front of a soft background. This isolation ability plus its ideal focal length for people pictures make it an excellent portrait lens. Also, new from Nikon is the 105mm f/2.0 D AF DC portrait lens with variable soft-focus effects.

Telephoto Lenses

Most photographers think about buying a telephoto lens with the idea that they bring distant subjects closer. Telephoto lenses do serve this purpose, but that is only one of many things for which telephoto lenses are useful.

When a telephoto lens design is combined with a wide aperture, the possibility of working with extremely shallow depth of field allows the creation of very interesting images. This is often spoken of as the isolation ability of the lens. This characteristic can be used to great advantage in wildlife, sports and outdoor portrait photography.

Another important use for telephoto lenses is that they compress perspective. You have seen this effect often in the movies when a long distance view of a crowded street makes it look like all of the people are crammed in together, when in fact they are separated by several feet. The same effect is often seen in cityscapes taken from the tops of buildings in which all of the buildings seem stacked up against each other. Telephoto lenses also alter perspective by making background objects larger in proportion to the main subject, this effect is often used in fashion photography.

Nikon's 180mm f/2.8N ED-IF AF is a lens in this range that I recommend. Thanks to an internal focusing mechanism, it can not only be focused very quickly by the autofocus system, but also has particularly high optical quality.

Super Telephoto Lenses

At any sporting event you see them, rows of super telephoto lenses from the press corps. Whether it is football, baseball, soccer, tennis, swimming, auto-racing, or any other sport which requires magazine and newspaper coverage, they are there. For the average photo hobbyist these large super telephotos are dream lenses, but for the professional photojournalist they are the tools of the trade.

Super telephotos are useful for the same reasons as telephotos, only their effects are even more pronounced. Compression is greater, depth of field is shallower at a given aperture, and it is possible to isolate a smaller subject from distracting surroundings. This is the reason that many nature photographers use these lenses. Most of them own one or more of these big lenses and carry them into the field for spectacular photos of animals and birds. All of these photographers curse the weight and size of the lenses, but use them because nothing else will produce the quality of photos on which their reputation depends.

Nikon has a truly super lens in the 300mm f/2.8 ED-IF AF. It is the large, expensive lens that you see on the television being used by photojournalists and sports photographers. A lighter, more compact and less expensive alternative is the 300mm f/4.0 ED-IF. While it is not as fast as the f/2.8 lens, its optical quality is just as good.

Zoom Lenses

Zoom lenses got a bad reputation in their early days due to the fact that the first zoom lenses were pretty bad by anyone's standards. Today, thanks to many technological innovations on the part of Nikon engineers, we have high quality zoom lenses which rival the best fixed focal length lenses.

One zoom lens can replace a number of fixed focal length lenses. For example the 75-300mm f/4.5-5.6 AF incorporates the fixed focal lengths of 85mm, 105mm, 135mm, 180mm, 200mm and 300mm. This versatility is what makes the zoom a powerful, creative tool for the photographer. It makes zooms very economical to own as well, eliminating the need to purchase all of these lenses separately.

Using a zoom properly requires that the photographer be very observant since zooms often will capture unwanted objects in the scene. It is easy to eliminate these however, since a zoom can simply be zoomed in or out to recompose the image. When using a zoom on a camera, such as the N6006 or N8008s, that provides only 92% viewing, not all of the image captured on the film is actually seen in the viewfinder. With these cameras, zooming wider to see and discover any unwanted elements, then zooming back to eliminate them is the way to double check the final image.

In the normal range, the 28-70mm f/3.5-4.5 AF is a zoom designed for the photographer who shoots with a camera with built-in flash such as the N6006. Larger lenses tend to cut-off of the camera's built-in flash, creating a dark line in the photograph. The small size of the 28-70mm eliminates this problem which is why it was added to the Nikon system.

In the longer zoom range, the 70-210mm N AF's small, compact size, ease of use and economical price, make it extremely popular. The change from a fixed f/stop to a variable f/stop accounts for its smaller size. All versions of this lens have excellent sharpness. This is especially true in the corners which is not typical for zooms. It has a macro mode providing a 1:4.5 magnification. The AF 80-200mm ED f/2.8 is expensive, but also of incredible quality. It is mechanically solid, offers exceptionally smooth manual focusing, but is rather cumbersome and heavy.

Macro Lenses

Macro lenses, or "micro lenses," as Nikon calls them, are designed to focus sharply on a flat subject, such as a document to be copied, and provide sharp focus in the center and at all four corners. Most lenses are not designed for such critical purposes and have a concave plane of focus. In general photography this matters little, and we do not normally even notice it, but it is disastrous for critical close-up copy work. That is why if you intend to do a lot of copy work, you should buy a true macro lens and not try to make do with a normal or zoom lens fitted with close-up accessories.

One of the first lenses Nikon ever manufactured was a micro lens. The 60mm f/2.8 AF carries on Nikon's long commitment to this specialized area of photography but with a new innovation in that it is able to go 1:1 without the use of an extension tube. It carries on the high standards of previous micros for sharpness and performance.

The 1:1 magnification is accomplished by an internal rearrangement of the lens elements which move and change their relationship to each other. In this way, extension does not need to be added to the rear of the lens to achieve 1:1 magnification as it is accomplished internally.

For subjects such as live insects which often require more space for lighting or to not frighten them away, the 105mm micro is more useful. It will also focus all the way to 1:1 without the need for extension tubes. Precise focus is very important in macro photography because the depth of field is quite shallow at high magnification and subject or camera movement is magnified. Use of the depth of field preview (N8008s only) is important in this sort of photography to insure that the depth of field is sufficient.

PC Lenses

These lenses are used in architectural photography. Their optics actually "shift" to avoid converging lines, making the images look more realistic. When using a shift lens, you can shoot from a low angle and from a relatively close distance without worrying about distortion.

Such complicated optics are obviously not compatible with the N6006/N8008/s autofocus system. You can use the PC 28mm f/3.5 and PC 35mm f/2.8 in "M" or "A" exposure modes, with center-weighted or spot metering. If you plan to invest in one of these specialized lenses, I recommend buying the 28mm, simply because in many instances the 35mm's perspective is just not wide enough.

Non-Nikkor Lenses

Nikon has a particularly good range of AF lenses available. You may, however, wish to explore the options offered by other companies. It is important to note, however, that while Nikon guarantees flawless performance of its lenses, such a guarantee does not necessarily come with lenses made by other manufacturers. If you purchase a Nikon-compatible lens from a reputable manufacturer (Tamron, Tokina, Vivitar and Sigma are just a few), the performance will be good. These firms have been in the photographic industry for many years, and offer good optics plus, reliable and fairly quick warranty repairs.

Both Tamron and Sigma offer a wide range of Nikon-compatible autofocus lenses. Sigma has a 28-70mm f/3.5-4.5, a fast 75-200mm f/3.8, and a particularly brilliant 70-210mm f/3.5-4.5 APO. Their fixed focal length 24mm f/2.8 and Macro 90mm f/2.8 (stepless to 1:2, using the included closeup filter, 1:1) are worth considering. A runner-up is the relatively economical 400mm f/5.6.

Tamron offers a 35-90mm f/4-5.6, a 90-300mm f/4.5-5.6, an ultra-compact 28-200 f/3.8-5.6, a continuous-focus macro 90mm f/2.5, a 35-105mm f/2.8 constant aperture, a 70-210mm f/2.8, and a 300mm f/2.8.

Teleconverters

There is a wide range of accessories available from Nikon to enhance the performance of your camera and lens. One of the most popular of these is the teleconverter. Teleconverters fit between the camera body and lens and effectively increase the focal length of the lens. For example, Nikon's most popular model, the TC-16A, increases the focal length by a factor of 1.6; a 200mm lens, used with the TC-16A, becomes a 320mm. The effective maximum aperture, however, becomes smaller, and the image quality of a lens with a converter is always a bit lower than the same lens without one. Nevertheless, for most applications, the image quality produced with a teleconverter is perfectly acceptable. Nikon has recently introduced AF-I teleconverters which are designed to allow Nikon autofocus systems to control non-autofocus lenses.

Macro Accessories

Extension Tubes

The extension tubes that are compatible with the N6006 and N8008/s are the PZ-11A, PK-12 and PK-13. The PK-11 is not, so be very careful when making a purchase. Extension tubes do their job, but macro lenses and close-up lenses are easier to use and more flexible.

Close-up Filters

Close-up filters, sometimes called diopters, are the least expensive macro photography option. When screwed onto the threaded filter mount of the lens, they shorten the minimum focusing distance. You can, therefore, get closer to your subject and increase the magnification ratio. Even get a 1:1 ratio is possible, depending on the lens and filter combination. Nikon makes close-up lenses with +0.7, +1.5 and +3 diopter in 52mm. I particularly recommend the multi-element close-up lenses, called 5T or 6T which Nikon offers in +1.5 and +2.9 diopters in both 52mm and 62mm sizes.

When using closeup lenses, you should stop down the lens as much as possible. This will help compensate for the natural reduction in quality from the close-up filter. Also, depth of field is so minimal in macro photography that stopping down will improve the quality of the entire image. Using a good tripod is also recommended.

Accessories

Focusing Screens for the N8008s

The N8008s can be equipped with two different screens. The standard screen which comes with the camera is the Type B It has a matte/fresnel field with only the autofocus bracket, small circle around it to indicate spot metering and large circle to indicate center-weighted metering.

Type B Screen: This screen is specially designed for AF cameras. It is similar to the standard focusing screen in the N6006 but without the spilt-image or microprism. It is fresnel ground and has markings for the AF measuring field, a 12mm reference circle for center-weighted metering and, depending on camera model, a reference circle for spot metering. The matte 12mm circle is useful for manual focusing in close-ups or with fast telephoto lenses.

Type E Screen: This is the same as the Type B screen except it has five vertical and three horizontal lines. This screen is often referred to as the architectural screen as vertical lines can be lined up with it. But it is most often used to keep the horizon straight and as a composition aid.

Eye Cups

Eye cups, made of black rubber, shield the viewfinder from side light. The cup also prevents exposure errors caused by stray light that enters the viewfinder around the eye.

Eyepiece Correction Lenses

Nikon cameras come standard with a built-in -1 diopter. This lens should allow fatigue-free viewing. For those whose eyesight requires correction, diopters from -5 to +3 in full steps (except for +0.5) are available. *User tip:* A correction lens should be selected to render optimal sharpness when used in conjunction with the visual aids (glasses or contact lenses) the photographer usually wears.

Cable Releases

A cable release is a useful tool in copy work, macro photography or in any long exposure situation because it releases the shutter without shaking the camera. Portraits from a tripod are made easier since they allow the photographer to interact directly with the subject face to face, as opposed to having one's head always behind the camera. If a cable release is not available and the precise time of the exposure is not critical, the self-timer can be used as a replacement. The N6006 takes a classic cable release, the N8008s takes the MC-12A electronic release.

Lens Hoods

Lens hoods should be used at all times to prevent stray light from striking the front lens element. This extraneous light can cause flare, ghosts and/or sun spots. Lens hoods also offer some protection from front-end collisions.

Nikon lens hoods come in four types: screw-in, snap-on, slip-in and built-in. These are designed to match the angle of view of the lens for maximum protection against stray light.

Care should be taken that the hood does not show up in the photograph. This is easy to do: install the hood on the lens and, while looking through the viewfinder, use the depth of field preview (N8008s) to stop the lens down to its smallest opening. When looking at a bright, uniform area, like a clear sky, make sure there is no light falloff at the corners.

It is also easy to detect if a hood does not offer enough protection from glare. Repeat the above test, but this time place a finger on the front edge of the hood and slide it into the field of view. It is best to place the finger in a position so that when it comes into view it will be in the corner of the viewfinder. When you can first see your finger, stop moving it and decide if you had to move it much before it could be seen.

A good hood offering maximum protection would allow almost no finger movement in the above test; a hood that is too wide for the lens it is being tested with will allow quite a lot of finger movement. Also be sure to test the hood with a filter in place between it and the lens, if you plan to use filters in conjunction with that hood, otherwise the test is invalid. In other words, the extra thickness of the filter plays an important part in the match and testing of a hood. The tests described here cannot be performed with N6000-series cameras because they lack a depth of field preview feature. Shooting a test roll of film is recommended instead.

Filters

Filters are among the useful accessories because they solve many of the problems that arise between film and the quality of light. Professionals are well aware of their purposes and use them when needed. Nikon manufactures filters only in the sizes that fit Nikkor lenses; I have included the Nikon designations in the headers. This is a brief list, for more information, contact your dealer.

UV or Skylight Filters LIBC, L37, L37C, L39
UV and Skylight filters not only provide the front element with protection against fingerprints and scratches, but also cut out harmful UV rays. The skylight filter also just slightly warms a scene because of its pink color. Many photographers leave these filters on their lenses at all times to protect against damage to the lens' front element.

Polarizing Filters
Polarizing filters can eliminate distracting reflections on non-metallic surfaces such as water, glass, polished stone, wood or varnished surfaces, as well as dyed surfaces. Also, grasses, plants and (in particular in southern countries) plants with leather-like leaves not only reflect visible light but also UV radiation which the film receives as blue light. In these situations, polarizing filters produce warm, spring-like green colors. The effect is strongest at an angle between 30 and 40 degrees relative to the reflecting surface. Longer focal lengths enhance this effect significantly. Distance views are improved in particular. The effect of a polarizing filter may be adjusted while looking through the viewfinder. Circular polarizers (as opposed to linear) should always be used with autofocus cameras.

Neutral Density Filters
Neutral density filters cut back the amount of light reaching the

film without altering the color or tonal rendition of a scene. Graduated neutral-density filters, like polarizing filters, are a "must" for landscape photographers in order to reduce intense contrasts produced by the sky. Water, sky, snow and sand or other light-colored surfaces can also be darkened with these filters. Colorless subjects (such as sky) benefit from colorization and darkening. Cokin® makes many different filters of this type.

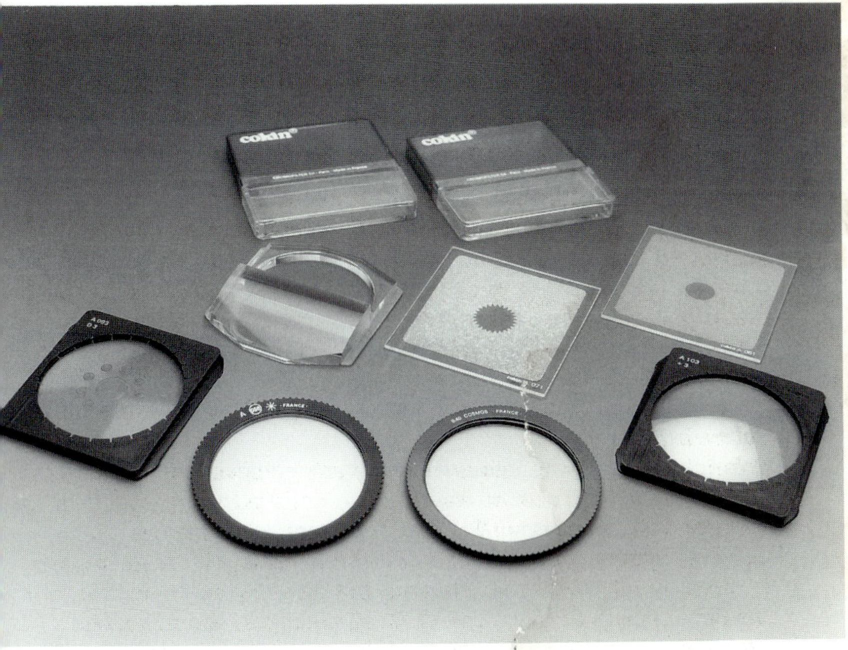

A variety of special effects filters from Cokin. PHOTO: Mike McWilliams

Filters for Black and White Photography

With all black and white filters, subjects of the same color as the filter become lighter and complementary-color subjects become darker. This effect can be used to alter the way colors are reproduced on the gray-scale or to increase contrast between two colors which would otherwise be rendered as a similar shade of gray.

Yellow Filter Y44, Y48, Y52

This filter is used to produce a tonally correct sky. It is a must to obtain correct tones in sunny snowscapes.

Orange Filter O56

This filter darkens blues. White clouds stand out vividly against the sky. Views of distant objects are enhanced. Its effect may be increased dramatically by adding a polarizing filter.

Red Filter R60

With this filter, blue sky turns deep black, clouds are offset distinctly and everything red will become considerably lighter.

Special Effect Filters

These filters, by manufacturers such as Cokin®, represent a broad cross-section of effects, from multi-image prisms to dazzling color effects and unusual distortions. The choice of using such filters is up to the photographer since these filters are not necessary to correct the light quality as with correction and conversion filters. Some photographers use them freely while others avoid them altogether. Many of these filters are dependent on the focal length used, the focus distance, the space between the filter and the front element, the aperture, the contrast, etc. etc. In short, the possible applications and variations are endless. It should be noted, however, that these filters may require placing the camera in a manual focus and/or manual exposure mode because of the way they affect camera and lens functions.